I0141955

Men

An Owner's Manual

ISBN-13: 978-0988399006
ISBN-10: 0988399008

Acknowledgements

Jacquelyn Jones – Her help with copyedit was invaluable. Her suggestions, comments, and input helped me stay out of the dog house with my wife.

Charles Mwalimu, PhD. Social Scientist – His proofreading skills caught everything, which is remarkable considering he had tears in his eyes from laughing so hard while he was reading this.

Men – Thanks for inadvertently helping me write this book by doing the things we do.

A special thanks to my wife.

For all the years we've been up and down,

For all the years we've been in and out,

I hope the years to come are filled with love,

I also hope they're not filled with Gout.

I love you,

Love Neil

Foreword

I have had the distinct and humble pleasure to read through the raw manuscript of *Men: An Owner's Manual* by "Lord Neil Robert" (He has a Seal issued by the Principality of Sealand that states he is Lord Neil Robert). This piece of information should alert anyone reading this book how funny and humorous Neil approaches life. Yet he is a very serious person with a very serious message about human nature and building viable relationships between women and men.

Neil tells the story in such a very hilarious fashion, that the book should disarm even his most ardent detractors especially men planning to relieve him of his "Man Card."

As noted above, Neil is fun, but not funny. He is one serious gentleman. His book is funny and yet with a very fundamental message, how to live life seriously with your mate without taking yourselves too seriously, and not to lose sight of daily perspectives of how you fell in love with each other to begin with.

The humor is self deprecating without being offensive. The lessons are relevant to all men and women of any age, especially those starting their journeys in searching for mates, in particular a long term mate.

In a way the book is about a very beautiful love story between Neil and his beloved wife. It is a pure love lived through various struggles of life but triumphs in the end. And the journey is not over for the couple. It is truly a splendid way Neil says "I Love you" to his beloved wife. He does not care if anyone else in the world knows about this love story.

It is a must read for all women of all ages. It is also a must read for all men of all ages unless indeed "they are in need of training." If this be the case, try the book anyway, it will make your training session easier. Enjoy the book. It is a great read. Have fun with life reading the book laughing at yourself. But the subject of women and how they should appropriately be treated by every man with dignity honor and love is a serious subject. Neil handles it very well.

Charles Mwalimu

September 25, 2012

Table of Contents

Prerequisites to enjoy this book
(Parts list)

Before we begin on our journey dissecting the actions, thoughts, and habits of men, there are a few things you will need.

1. A sense of humor. You must be able to laugh at others but more importantly, laugh at yourself.
2. Patience. This manual is not meant to be read out of order. Each chapter builds on the last to piece together a more complete picture.
3. The ability to learn. There are plenty of suggestions contained inside. It is up to you to follow them.
4. An understanding this book is not written for men, but about men by a man. This book is about how we think, and why we do those things we do.
5. The comprehensive ability to grasp the reality not all men are created equal. We don't mimic each other and act the same way in similar situations. Given this simple guidance, I will be talking in generalities unless otherwise noted.
6. Complete knowledge of the working parts on a man. Remember, not all parts on a man work the way a woman thinks they should. I'll explain this further a few pages later.

7. A great bottle of wine. It sure can't hurt to be relaxed.

If you are a man reading this book, heed number one above. If you chose to ignore my advice, you will become mad, upset, denounce my very existence and probably stalk me with malicious intent.

If you are a woman reading this book, understand you will not believe a substantial amount of what's written. It will be very hard for you to wrap yourself around my advice, but trust me on this, if you take the training here semi seriously, you'll be amazed at the results.

So, who should read this book?

Everyone, I hope. This book is written by an ordinary man about men. It is also written for anyone who enjoys a humorous look at the "not so complex" behavior of the common man. Think of this book as a "how to train your man" manual for women. I decided to write this book because I was tired of seeing books about men written by women or written by an over-educated man who never had his butt kicked or hung out in local bars.

The stories and advice I'm going to share are from my personal experience, my personal observations or events told to me by other men. I use my wife and I as examples in most situations I describe. That does not mean it is my story, it means I'm not telling if the story is mine or someone else's.

I have been told by several men that I will lose my "Man Club" card over this book. So be it.

I cannot say this enough, but men will not react the same way in the exact same situation. I will be repeating this throughout the book. It's that important.

What else will you need to fully enjoy this book?

Nothing else. You already have all the tools you need built in. You just need to know how to use them most effectively on men.

Now, get your glass of wine, sit back and relax. You're in for eye opening revelation about the common man and how to train him.

Chapter 1

In the beginning...

Men are dogs. That's right; I said it and I'll stand by it. The way we act, our actions and gestures are all very similar to that of a dog. The sooner we understand and accept this statement, the easier it will be to convert your man from a dog into a stallion.

To understand man the species, you have to understand whence we came. To put it in plain English, "where we been." Understanding our past will answer many questions.

Evolution and creationism are two schools of thought on how humans became to exist. I will not take sides as to which theory is right or wrong, but will discuss my take on both.

We'll start with creationism.

God created Adam in his own image. Soon God realized Adam would be a mental patient if he didn't have a companion. God gave Adam a choice. God is all about freewill and choice.

God said, "Give up a rib and I'll give you a mate, a companion, a woman." Adam had no idea what a woman was, not sure if he wanted to know and since Adam had been eating nothing but fruits and nuts, which he likes, wasn't sure he would like the taste of woman. Adam wasn't quick to agree mainly because of the whole "Give up a rib" thing. Even though Adam didn't know what a rib was, it sounded unpleasant having to give one up. Here's where man started having trouble sharing. So Adam asked God what was behind door number two.

God said, "I'll give you eternal happiness if you promise to never question my guidance, my wisdom and my eternal love for you." Here is where the freewill part comes into play. Not wanting to limit his options, Adam asked God if there was a third choice. God became angry and then asked Adam the rhetorical question, "Are you an idiot?" God realized that he would have to make the choice for Adam after realizing Adam had no sense.

God took Adams rib and presto, woman was created. God told Adam she would be called "Eve."

Adam liked the look of Eve very much. He liked the smell, the feel, the nice things she would say to him, and he liked the taste. Yes, he bit into her trying to find out if she was food.

Adam was content and very grateful to God for the wonderful creature God created. He thanked God by being a loyal dog, always being there when God called.

God wanted to reward Adam for his loyalty so he created animals. He explained that Adam would have dominion over the animals. Eve was not pleased by this directive from the head office. She felt she should have equal rights and could care for the animals as good as, if not better, than Adam. Discontent began to take root in the garden.

In the process of creating an animal kingdom for Adam to care for, the lawyer was created. I'm sure the lawyer fell through the quality control section and disguised himself as a snake.

Adam and Eve are kicking back in the Garden of Eden completely bored out of their minds. After all, there are only a few things to do in the garden. Sex has not been discovered yet, so there goes the best 10 minutes of each day.

God warned Adam and Eve not to eat the fruit from tree of knowledge. He explained it would cause great unrest within the tranquility of the kingdom and could change the very fabric of nature.

Eve, still stewing over the animal thing, begins to eye the Tree of Knowledge. Adam, sensing the frustration in Eve, reminds her of the guidance God has given both of them.

Along comes the snake. He slithers along-side of Eve and whispers in her ear the fruit on that beautiful tree is tasty and full of juice. He suggests it can't be too bad to just try a bite. When Eve speaks of the wrath of God for eating from the tree, the snake simply says, "God's not looking right now."

As time passed, Eve became more disillusioned with Adam, the whole Garden of Eden thing and God. She decided the snake was right. She asked herself "What harm could be done by trying a small bite?"

Eve walked to the tree and picked an apple from a low hanging branch. Not wanting to be the only one to get in trouble if God did happen to notice the indiscretion, Eve, with some prodding from the snake, decided Adam would need to try it with her.

You see, if Eve had just listened to God, this book wouldn't be necessary. Man would still be ignorant and naïve, while woman would be a pleasant distraction from the animals.

Eve began to eat the apple from the tree of knowledge. She took one bite and was instantly transformed from a "pleasant distraction" to "Eve, The Goddess of Appetite." Although at this time, Adam had still not partaken in the fruit he had no knowledge of her true beauty. Eve continued to eat and with each bite became more knowledgeable and understanding in the ways of the world.

The snake reminded Eve share this true delight with Adam. Eve, having gained some knowledge at this point, going against her feelings, decided to offer Adam a small portion. Thereby not only giving Adam some knowledge but also making him an accomplice after the fact in breaking God's only rule, "Thou Shalt Not Eat My Fruit."

Just for the record, Eve FORCED Adam to eat the fruit (I know this because everyone knows a woman can get a man to do almost anything if she shows a little cleavage). That's right, Eve forced Adam. Up to this point, Adam hadn't had an original thought of his own and was very content frolicking in the garden, playing with the animals and occasionally including Eve in the festivities.

Eve ate most of the fruit and when there was only a bite or so left, she shared the scraps with Adam. He took one or two bites and had nothing but the core to nibble on.

By eating most of the fruit and only saving the core for Adam, Eve inadvertently consumed most of the knowledge contained within. This enlightenment consisted of emotion, kindness, selfless sacrifice and sensitivity which, among others, were the qualities Eve secured for all women. What were left were only small traces of those qualities but the most important of qualities was only contained in the core, wisdom. Eve did get a taste of wisdom, but most of it was consumed by Adam. Adam received "The leftovers" of the aforementioned qualities, but the division of knowledge was most definitely skewed in Eve's favor.

The division by Eve of the apple's power should explain why men think the way they do.

Although it was Eve who broke God's rule, God took it out on both of them. The snake was spared God's wrath save for the decree the snake must always remain a lawyer or a politician.

God decided to punish Adam and Eve for their transgression. He cursed Eve with the ability to have multiple orgasms but the inability for man to give them to her. God also bestowed on her the ability to give birth. Now you know the answer to the question of "Why can only women give birth? They deserve it."

For Adam, God reserved a special damnation. Knowing Eve FORCED Adam to partake, God decided to give Adam the gift of marriage and erectile dysfunction, in that order.

After a few days of getting acquainted with these new feelings, Eve walked to where Adam was sitting. He wasn't thinking, he wasn't doing anything, but sitting. I know most women don't understand this concept of actually being devoid of thought, but men can produce nothing very easily. So Eve walked over to Adam and asked the first question recorded in history. Yes, she started it. I know this because men don't ask questions, we don't read instructions, and we don't ask for directions.

Eve asked Adam the single question which will haunt all men for all eternity, "Why?"

The question of "Why?" is unanswerable as-is. It can't be debated or argued. You can never rally for or against it. If you agree, you're wrong, if you disagree, you're wrong. I believe this is the motivation behind why philosophy professors always put that question on their first exam they give during the first year of college. It is one of very few questions which have no answer, yet millions try to force an answer to it.

Well, Eve asked "Why?" and expected an answer. This caused great confusion for Adam. He pondered for a moment and answered, "What?"

Eve asked the question once more. Adam, completely confused, answered with, "What the hell are you talking about?"

A hint for men; you never answer a woman's question with a question, especially if that woman is the only other person in your world.

This is lesson one for women. Don't confuse your man with questions which have no answer. Also, don't get mad when your man answers what he thinks you're truly asking, or when he answers with a question which helps him clarify what your question is about.

As life went on and time passed, Adam and Eve (having lived in the same tree house for a while) became less interested in each other. Eve began to explore her womanhood as Adam explored his manhood.

One day Eve became so frustrated with Adam (she caught him not thinking again), she started yelling at him. This was something new for Adam. He stood there bewildered at the tone of her voice, the swing in emotions she displayed and the language she was using. He had no choice but to yell back at her. This just infuriated Eve to her boiling point. She yelled at Adam, "You never listen to me." At this point, she demanded Adam move out of the tree house. She demanded from God an explanation for why her body kept playing tricks on her. She asked God why wasn't Adam able to listen to what she was saying and, what was the meaning of life. God, not wanting to piss Eve off even more than she was, explained in order of the questions, "Menopause, because you're screaming at him and none of your business."

At the same time, Adam was standing on the ground below the tree house. This was his first experience with fear. He kept calling to Eve asking if he could come up and get his things. Adam had very little possessions, but he did have a few fig leaves to cover himself up. After all, after they both ate the apple, modesty and humility were the first few emotions they felt.

The entire time the snake was curled up next to Eve giving her advice regarding how to handle Adam and his requests. Eve kept repeating to Adam what the snake was telling her, "You can have your fig leaves when you pry them from my cold, dead, hands" was one of the things she yelled at Adam.

Adam picked up a rock and threw it at the snake. Adam missed the snake. This was a big mistake. Adam hit Eve in the middle of the head which left a huge mark on her forehead. I swear he did not throw the rock at Eve.

Having seen this, the snake immediately called upon God and said, "See what your creation has done. He has injured the gift you gave him and desecrated this holy place with violence."

God listened to both sides before passing judgment. God decided both Adam and Eve could no longer live in the same tree house. God gave Eve the tree house and custody of the snake. He gave Adam his fig leaves and ordered Adam to provide food for Eve on a daily basis for the next five years or until Eve finds another Adam to shack up with, whichever came first. God also put Adam in an anger management class and made him serve 240 hours of garden clean up service.

God decided he needed a few more rules to guide humanity. He came up with the Six Commandments. The

Ten Commandments didn't come about until much later. God realized a few more rules were needed in addition to some amendments of the current Commandments.

As it turned out, Eve was not dealing with menopause, she was pregnant, and this would change the world as they knew it.

Now that we have explored creationism, let's take a look at Evolution.

Although there were many people in societies around the world subscribing to the Theory of Evolution, very few would express it publicly. Evolution has only been a mainstream debate for the last six decades or so. Let's take a look at what the "Evolutionists" aren't telling you.

As the earth evolved, a microbe developed from a water creature to an air breathing, land-dwelling creature. Hence, man crawled from the oceans onto land and took up residence in caves. The "caveman" was born.

As the caveman progressed though time, many other species were developing. The female humanoid developed, mainly out of a necessity for a companion for the male humanoid.

Historians will have you believe that the cave man would hit his mate over her head and then drag her back to his cave. Presumably to have his way with her. Well, I'm here to tell you it didn't happen that way at all. Men might be dense in some areas, but we know our history and this is the way it really went...

The caveman had already developed into an upright walking dominant force on the planet. Although there were many other species stronger than man, man alone had the gift of thought. It was this ability to think that made him take up residence in a cave.

She too had the gift of thought and took up residence in a much nicer cave. Her cave had pretty things hanging from the openings in the cave wall. She had animal hide lying across the floor of the cave so you wouldn't get your feet dirty if you entered. She had it made, well as far as cave dwelling goes.

Woman developed alongside man at about the same pace. Woman seemed to develop just a bit faster, but man didn't care. He liked the looks and the feel of woman so he decided he would keep it.

One day, man was just sitting around minding his own business, hanging out with other men completely devoid of thought. Women strolled by the pack, remember she developed faster than man, and decided she would have one of them for herself. She knew very little about men, but she knew she had built-in tools that would kill most men, and she knew how to use them.

Woman used every tool in her arsenal to get man's attention, but he was too busy doing nothing with his caveman buddies. She showed him the assets she possessed and explained the pleasures he would enjoy if he would just go to her cave. Our brave caveman was not falling for the old, "come to my cave" ploy. He listened to his buddies and ignored her. Man had thought, but I never said it was rational.

Woman, not wanting to, or not being accustomed to taking "No" for an answer, and she definitely didn't want her attributes to lose to a bunch of middle aged cavemen in the prime of her life (by the way, middle age back then was about fifteen years old), decided to consult the "Rock of Wisdom."

The "Rock" as those "In the know" would call it, was perched atop a giant mountain. To get up the mountain it was Treacherous travels traversing to the top (that took a while to come up with), or the six "T's" as those in the know would say. She packed everything she had for the twenty-minute trip to the top. Four changes of animal skins, two hair bone combs (just in case one broke) and 30 gallons of bug spray. The bugs were very big back then.

Once she made it to the top, she approached the Rock with reverence and humility. Not something woman was accustomed to, but nevertheless, she humbled herself before the Rock. She asked the all-knowing Rock, "How do I get my man?" The Rock gave her the answer, "Pay little to no attention to him. He will want what he cannot have." The Rock knew all. The Rock was also upset that man kept pissing on it as a joke, and so was more than willing to reveal how to manipulate a man to the woman. The Rock was getting even with man.

She climbed down the mountain with confidence she had all she needed to get her man. She had a completely different approach and armed with the knowledge of the Rock, she knew she could not fail.

As woman walked past the pack this time, she would shun them like a stale piece of mammoth meat.

This course of action taken by the woman began to work, and it worked well (damned Rock). Man started to feel unwanted, unattractive and confused. Man said to himself, "Deh Ugh Boo Gur Dah" which is roughly translated into "Me not like this feeling."

Man, being confused as usual, walked over to Woman trying to start up a conversation. His every attempt to regain her interest was deflected like a pro-bowl lineman in the playoffs. Nothing he tried was working. Everything he thought of (which wasn't much) was rebuffed by her. She ignored him constantly. This went on for a few weeks. He would make a pass, she would deflect it. Man's cave buddies started calling her, "Ga-Bu-Dim" meaning "Bitch." Men kept using ga-bu-dim to describe women, but over time it has just been shortened to bitch.

Man decided to consult the Rock of Wisdom himself. As he made the treacherous travels traversing to the top of the great mountain, he began to think. Thinking was not a strong point of man during this evolutionary period.

Man arrived at the Rock and noticed it had ear rings, make –up and little rocks at the base painted a pretty shade of blue. Man knew woman had been there first. In front of the rock was a small saber tooth tiger rug woman had lain down to kneel on. With a flash of insight, man refrained from urination on the great rock.

Man kneeled down and asked the Rock, "Rock, how do I get the girl?" The rock (grateful man didn't urinate on it) proclaimed man must shower her with gifts. Man must make her feel pretty, needed, appreciated and above all, loved. Man became very excited and rushed down the mountain (he should have stayed for more lessons) to impress his girl with this new knowledge.

The first thing man set out to do was shower her with gifts. He went hunting. Mainly because that's what men do, we kill things. Man tracked down a brontosaurus and with a single blow, felled the animal for his girl. He field dressed the animal and brought her back the biggest brontosaurus burgers she had ever seen.

She wanted nothing to do with him. She ate the food, said "thank you" and sent him on his way. Man begun to doubt the great Rock and the advice which was given. Man was an idiot.

Man went back to the Rock and exclaimed the advice didn't work. The Rock replied, "One gift does not make a shower!" The Rock sent Man back to try again with the motto, "try, and try again."

Man devised a plan to give until he could give no more. He would give until it hurt, real bad. Give until she bowed to his will (well, that last part I added, but we know he was thinking it). Man began the plan by taking a bath. He really needed it and, as he discovered, it felt good too. Man gave woman pretty flowers and pretty stones. He could tell woman was starting to bend in his favor. He knew this because she didn't throw the stones at him.

After several nights of trying to impress her, climbing the highest tree, swinging from the highest branch, holding his breath under water longer than all others, he came up with the one thing woman didn't have, something she really wanted, and, man could steal it with the greatest of ease,

Fire. That's right, fire was the deal clincher. Although man had to steal fire, nobody could prove he stole it because all fire looked alike. Who's to say man didn't make it himself? That's our story and we're sticking to it.

Well, man succeeded in wooing woman (to her knees). She was his for him alone to command (as long as the fire stayed lit).

Much time passed and Man thought everything was fine. Man brought home the food, woman kept a clean cave. Occasionally she would change the writing on the cave wall so her man would not get bored staring at the same old thing. Life seemed it couldn't get any better, or so man thought.

Man was out with his buddies, they were bowling, in a strip club, with naked midgets. Completely harmless and innocent from man's point of view (and it was a good view). Woman just happened to be walking by (So she says. We think she was spying on man), when she saw her man's wheel parked out front of the cave bar. She went inside and noticed her man with two midgets wearing almost nothing and it appeared he was getting ready to "bowl" with them.

Man's buddy saw her walk in and he quickly changed positions with man (that's a true friend). She was not fooled. Woman walked up to man and asked if he planned on coming back to the cave with her. Not wanting to appear as a "kept" man, he declined and said, "I'll be home when I'm good and ready. Now get me a beer."

Woman was very happy with the answer. Especially the "Beer" part as distilled spirits hadn't been invented yet; she thought he wanted her to go out a kill a "Bear" as in animal. She also didn't want to embarrass him in front of his buddies, so she asked a simple question. Yes, the one question which has haunted all men since recorded time, "Why?"

Again, I must say I have no idea what possesses a woman to always ask that question. I've tried to figure it out and have not come up with a reasonable answer.

Not wanting to appear inferior to woman, man responded with, "What was that, honey?" We all know that response. It's the response men give everyone when they are trying to pretend they didn't hear the question. Woman knew this response well and she didn't like it. It made her feel she was being marginalized.

Woman had made the mistake of trying to exert her superiority in front of man's pals. In front of his pack, his gang, his peers, she called him a "bum."

Cavemen was now feeling his cave manhood challenged. He grabbed the closest thing, which just happened to be a log, and Wham!!! Hit her right on the head. He knocked her out quicker than a midget going down on bowling pins.

The other cave buddies, not having a woman of their own, saw this as a quick way to get the girls. The first date rape drug was invented; "The Club" I believe this is also where the phrase, "Going to the Club" started. You see, historians have it all wrong regarding hitting women over the head. It all started to shut up a single woman nagging at her man in front of his buddies.

Man, having knocked his mate unconscious, dragged her back to their cave. He realized the error of his actions long before she woke up. When she awoke from the trauma induced sleep, she was amazed to find the cave completely clean. The dishes were done, the place was spotless. She was pissed at him. No amount of "ass kissing" was going to make that go away.

During this time, one of man's buddies saw an opportunity present itself. The buddy approached the woman and convinced her to separate from man. He offered to counsel her for one third of her food. The buddy became the first "lawyer," so to speak. Some buddy he turned out to be.

Woman threw man out of the cave and told him never to come back. This is when she threw the pretty rocks at him from earlier. Man's buddy had the Rock of Wisdom summon both parties to the mountain top. The Rock was going to decree a resolution to the conflict.

Both parties made the treacherous travels traversing to the top of the mountain. The Rock decreed man would lose the cave, have to provide food to woman for a period of five years or when she "shacked" up with another caveman, whichever came first. Man would also have the cave kids every other Wednesday and on weekends.

After reading both scenarios, you might be wondering what either of them has to do with present-day man. It demonstrates our earliest thought patterns of who we are. Although man started as a free, thoughtless creature with little ambition, he was transformed by woman's actions. It was woman who wanted man to think, to have emotion, be fearless and have strength. Woman received what she asked for. The lesson is to be careful of what you ask for, you might just get it.

From the time men are children, they are taught strength and power are synonymous, they must be rough and tough and that real men don't cry. Once we reach the teenage years, these traits are reinforced by the behavior of the teenage girl. It isn't until we reach manhood that all our training becomes twisted. What we have learned as boys seems to be wrong, which that is confusing for us, as men.

Women want a tender man, one who understands romance and the strength of passion. If women would understand the concept, "men don't cry," it would be easier for women to undo the bad training men have had since childhood.

Men still have the primitive instinct to hunt, be fearless, and be strong at all costs. It comes naturally to men. You can see this when you go to a bar. Men go on the prowl, looking for the one girl who'll be easy prey for his charms and wit. As his buddies watch, he becomes fearless on the hunt, brushing aside any rejection with laughable indignation.

Our genetic composition as men still has not discarded our primordial instincts as cavemen or Adam. Men tend to regress when around other men. We tend to display a false persona of strength and wisdom, power and intelligence. This can be compared to male animals peeing in their territory or the alpha male in a pack exerting his dominance over the other members of the pack.

Next time you're in a bar, watch a group of men. You'll see behavior which resembles a litter of lion cubs vying for the title of leader and to acquire the affections and attentions of all around.

Keep in mind, this is not reversible. No amount of training can extinguish the display.

In both creation and evolution, man makes progress. Since the beginning, man has progressed much. I'm not sure how much, but I am sure we have learned some things. But you must be aware that because we have made some progress on the evolutionary ladder, we have the ability to regress. This is a real threat we must constantly be on the lookout for.

This book is about the average man, not the man who has moved forward, not the man who makes a difference in the world. We are not talking about the great thinkers or the inventors of time and space. These are the men who truly make an impact on humanity. This book is not about them.

I know there are plenty of women who have made an impact on our world also, yeah, yeah, yeah, blah, blah, blah, this book is about men and why we do those inexplicable things we do.

We should all take a moment to reflect on the origins of man, okay, time's up. Let's get on with the rest of the book.

Chapter 2

The Language of Man

In the first chapter you learned the true beginnings of man. I know most people will disagree with me, especially historians. Remember, most historians are men, and therefore, the information is skewed to put man in a better light. To truly understand your man and help you in the difficult task of training him, you will need to understand his language.

This is not any language you could have learned in school. It is part of our genetic makeup, much like the secret language of women, however, in man's case it is instinctive. It is a language men are born with. We understand it from day one.

My wife of 20 plus years finally admitted to me something I have known for a long time. Women take a class, a secret class at age 12 which is designed to teach them their secret language. Then around age 25 or so, depending on the woman, take a refresher class. I knew this, I just couldn't prove it. Well, men are born with this ability to understand other men. We don't need a stinking class.

The language of man is not made up of distinguishable words. They are more along the lines of sounds and motion, noise and gestures, or as my wife put it, "baboon movements with the sound of heavy metal music playing at ten times speed." She really didn't put it that way, but I didn't like the way it came out so I had to blame someone and she got tagged for it.

I will try to explain to you how to communicate with your man. My therapist says communication is the key to a long and happy relationship. I disagree with her. The key to a long and happy relationship is not getting caught, taking separate vacations, having a hidden bank account. Those are things which give relationships stability. Stupid therapist, I tried to tell HER this, but she didn't listen. She then accused me of not listening to her and that started an entire new set of sessions. Sorry, I got side-tracked, back to the communication thing.

To communicate with your man, you must know how to speak "Man" and understand him when he speaks "Man." There are many sounds which all men will use, which if mastered by you, will make your instructor job much easier.

"Aaah," "Ooh," "Ah," "Errr," "Ughah" and "Huh"

Say these words with me. Good, you're now on your way to understanding our language.

Remember, mastering those sounds is imperative to successfully training your man. Just knowing how to say them is not enough. You're not a man and could never convey the same meaning as a man does when using those sounds. You should know how to say them, but more importantly, you need to know what they mean.

There are hundreds of definitions for each sound. Each sound is based on, and is dependent on, the gesture accompanying it and the pitch used when making it. Sometimes the sound will be used in conjunction with a facial expression. You must pay close attention whenever you hear any of those sounds and take note of his gestures so you don't miss cues as to their present context and meaning.

The language is too complex to explain all the interpretations. For that reason, I will give you examples of these sounds, but only a fraction of their use will be covered. Once you understand the basics, you should have no trouble figuring out the rest.

For instance, let's say your man is pointing at the TV and making the "Aaah" sound in a slightly elevated pitch, that means you're standing in front of the TV, you need to move because your ass is blocking the screen. If you're not standing anywhere near the TV, then it means he wants you to look at the TV because there is something on TV he wants or it's something he wants you to see. It could also mean he is out of beer and, because he's watching a program, he wants you to get him another on your way back from the kitchen. Meaning, you need to go to the kitchen and get him a beer.

Hey, don't get mad at me, your man is the one who said it. I'm just translating for you.

The frequently used, and the most basic sound men make is the hunger moan. The "Ughah" sound. This sound is always accompanied by specific gestures. It is only used to indicate hunger, nothing else. The gestures are unmistakable and are always the same with every man.

It begins with a prowling movement through the kitchen. A movement not unlike a wild animal stalking its prey. You've all seen it, now you know what it is called; "grazing."

This is where your man will look at everything in the refrigerator and pantry at least three times. We always look three times, because we can't remember what we saw five minutes ago. As we look at each item, we are thinking of three things.

First, how is it going to taste right now? Even though we may have had that item hundreds of times in the past, we need to know how it will taste now.

Second, do we want to go to all the trouble to make the food? If it requires a lot of time and prep to put together, we're probably going to pass.

Third and more importantly, how do we get you to make it for us? If we can come up with a way for you to cook for us, then it won't matter what we chose. Who cares, after all, you're the one cooking it.

Yes, we are thinking only of those three things. We will go through this process for each edible item. Although you should know, we are putting emphasis on the third thought.

Once a decision of what to eat is made, men will start making one of a few sounds. This sound will be similar to a pack of monkeys freaking out, just not so loud and in a bit of a lower pitch, perhaps like a growling tiger or a puppy crying. The sound your man will make will depend on how far your man has evolved, how much training he has had. The further up the evolutionary ladder your man is, the more similar to the crying puppy the noise will resemble.

Remember, this book is a "How-To" book which will help you push your man up the evolutionary ladder. The more time you put into his training, the further up the ladder he will progress (you like how I am able to put it all on you?) As the trainer, it is truly on you. You control the degree to which you want to elevate your man. But, be careful, if you evaluate your man beyond a certain level, there will be no controlling him.

When you hear the monkey's screeching, remember, it's just the noise we make once we have found what we want. Don't think a cat got run over in your driveway.

After we've decided, we'll usually pull the item and put it on the counter. We'll stare at it for another few minutes. We might even put it back and get something else. It's the second guess process. Very little noise will be made during this phase. All too often, the food we chose is not appropriate for the meal period. My wife will attest to this. Well, back to the sounds and gestures before I divulge the coming chapters.

There are many sounds and gestures like I said before. One of those sounds is not "Bitch, get my beer." This sound is very unique in that it represents a man who has never been trained. Your time and supervision will be tested with this man. After a few months, if your man has not stopped uttering this noise, it's time to leave him. The next woman might thank you for starting the ground work, but unless he gets more training soon, he'll have to start at step one all over again.

Another distinct sound is that of excitement, not to be confused with pleasure. This "excitement" sound is unique in tone to all other sounds, but will vary in pitch and inflection according to your man. It resembles the sound of a pack of dogs all going for the same ball. It translates to, "That is the coolest thing I ever saw", that is, until the next coolest thing comes along.

The sounds men make at gatherings are slightly harder to differentiate than most others. There is the "my cousin is looking better and better" sound which can't be translated into words. It's a slight sound, as we don't want anyone to hear us and conclude we're sick and need therapy. Gatherings are special for men. We see them as a chance to pick up girls, yes, even once-removed cousins. So the sounds are muted. We do this out of a natural instinct to survive.

The "Oh, Shit" sound is produced in a variety of ways, but at every family event you'll hear it more than ten times. The first time is usually when we see your parents, your brother or our grandmother.

Our grandmother is the worst of them. She's the lady pinching our cheek. We must stand there and take the punishment, hence the reason for the sound. We cannot squeeze grandma's cheek back, unless we want to put grandma in diapers for the rest of her life. But, I guess if she is already in diapers, it doesn't really matter.

Men make a treasure trove of sounds. These sounds will let you know if we're happy, sad, excited, hurt, depressed and aroused. Yes, aroused.

Unfortunately, this sound is the same for everyman. Yes, it's true; we all make the same sound. It's a car crash. The sound is not like a car crash, but I say it's a car crash in that it is something you can't look away from and you can't un-see or un-hear it. You have to see it and say, "Wow," to really take it all in (no pun intended).

The sooner you understand some of the basic sounds your man makes, the shorter your journey on the road to train your man will be. Spend time listening to his noises, watching his gestures accompanying those noise's and pay attention to what he is doing at the time of making both.

Remember, gestures and noises go hand in hand. The same sound may accompany several different gestures. The same gesture may accompany several different sounds.

The sounds and gestures that make up the communication between a mother and her baby are translated into unspoken language which transcends all other methods of communication.

It will take a new mother several months to figure out what her newborn wants by the noise it makes. Don't expect to understand your man in under that same time.

So pay attention and watch your man and you'll get the hang of his language soon.

Chapter 3

The Trained Dog...

Many women believe men are dogs. This isn't far from the basic truth of it. Most men are dogs. We have rejected the teachings of the wisest. Usually we date, get trained by someone not qualified to train us, and then we revert back to our basic nature, "Dogism. "

Just because you're a woman doesn't make you qualified to train a man. You too must be trained in the proper use of "Man" training techniques. Just as in training a dog, if your skill set is below par, your dog will revert to its primordial instincts and act like, well, a dog. If however you're well trained, then you'll have a better chance of ensuring your dog's training sticks. The same holds true when training your man.

There will be relapses, but the more proficient you are, the fewer relapses your man will have. As an example, take the following;

This is your first visit to your man's home or apartment. Remember, we are still bachelors. As bachelors, we use disposable everything. Dishes are the best example. Our mother went out and bought us our first set of dishes for our apartment. These are obviously not meant to be disposable, but they become "throw away" dishes after about five uses. This is because most men don't do dishes. So we eat off them until you can't see the color anymore, then, presto, they're disposable.

In the "Crash Pad" we have a bed, no frame, a milk crate or old wooden box as our coffee table, a couch we either found or was given to us by our parents and the most expensive TV we could buy. This is a clue as to our priorities. Take note.

Before you're allowed in the pad, we shove everything we own into the closet, we put any dirty dishes back in the cupboard, which is why you're not allowed to get your own glass. We'll get it for you; after all, we know what is clean and what is not. We won't vacuum, but we will pick up the stuff you can see on the floor or shove it under the couch. The TV, which sits atop the stack of bricks with a piece of wood lying across to support it, will be cleaned of any moisture rings left from glasses from the party we had the night before.

The single bean-bag chair sitting in the corner of the room will be fluffed up and turned over, as we're not entirely sure what went on last night, but we know that chair was a big part of it. Some men might actually have a nice couch, a real TV stand and a bed with sheets and all. I'm not going to talk about the bathroom here because I don't want to. The bathroom is bad, real bad. So don't plan on using it your first visit. You'd be wise to heed this advice.

We now have you in the "den of the loin," yes, we're that arrogant, or more appropriately referred to as the "Dog House." You've had a few moments to assess the accommodations and think to yourself, "there are possibilities" or you would have left by now. Men have no idea what will happen next, but we do know you're in charge from this point forward. You have to give us that much, we're not entirely dense, just a bit thick. Our mothers trained us better than this, but since we've moved into our own place, we have relapsed.

Men are primitive creatures who need, no, long to be loved like you would a dog. For this reason, men will begin to do or say whatever it takes to get you to spend the night. Men aren't totally in control of their actions at this point. Half of the time, we don't even remember what we've already tried to do to sway you, so we'll try the same things over and again. We're trying to be the man of your dreams at this moment, but lack the ability to listen to you long enough to find out what that is. We want to please you and give you the loving you deserve, but only during commercials and only if it's not a beer commercial.

We want what every dog wants, food, TV and sex (in order of importance.) Yes, dogs want to watch TV. We also want everything imaginable so long as there are no strings attached. If you don't believe me, take this test. The next time you're at his apartment or yours, make his favorite meal and put it on the table. Go into the bedroom and get naked. Call out to him stating you're naked and dinner is on the table. I bet he stops to grab a bite before he makes it to the bedroom.

Still don't believe me, add this to your test. After you've put food on the table, turn on the TV on your way to the bedroom. Nine times out of ten, he'll grab a bite and stop to see what's on the TV BEFORE he makes it to the bedroom, if he makes it to the bedroom at all. You might have to remind him where you are and why you're in the bedroom to begin with. I just proved the order of importance, so don't question me again.

Women should understand that what I've just described is fact. If women knew this going in, and I think most women do, then men and women would get along just a bit better at first and it wouldn't feel so awkward. Sometimes I think a dog is easier to train.

Within the first hour or less in most cases, you (the woman) has sized up the task you have ahead of you in training this dog and transforming him into a ...(music of angels playing in the background)...MAN.

I warn you to tread lightly into the first stages of training for now, if you push too hard at the beginning; you'll lose him forever and hence be referred to as the "The bitch I threw out." Men do have an image to uphold.

Remember, your first visit is not a training session, merely an assessment mission. You're there to determine if you want to invest the time and energy it could take to train this man, thus being able to go out in public together and marriage as the ultimate goal. We are assuming this is not the first time you have met, or the first time going out. We assume you have gone to dinner or done something else with him prior to you going to his place. If this is the first time you're going out with him, shit, you're a tramp, do you want to go out with me?

When I was dating, I never took a girl to my apartment the first time I went out with her. I didn't want her to know where I lived just in case she turned out to be some kind of stalker man-killing machine. I don't know any men who pick up women in bars and take them back to their place; they all go to a hotel.

So assuming this is not your first time going out, but the first time visiting his apartment, here are a few pointers to consider on your first visit;

1. Let him know the apartment is not bad. As a matter of fact, say it's nice. This might cause you to choke a bit, but don't worry, he'll be more than happy to perform the Heimlich maneuver if required. He'll know you're lying to him, but it won't matter. Remember his goal, the "sleep-over." You could tell him that you've been in worse places. I know this might make you sound like a tramp, but to him it's a sign of

encouragement. Take notice of his facial reaction to the compliment and listen to his words. If he says, "Gee, thanks," run like the wind. He's a caveman and will hit you over the head with his club. You might be asking how I know this, well; a real man has no idea how to answer that obvious lie and most times would say, "Sorry I didn't clean yet." Then you know he's trainable.

2. When he asks if you would like a drink, don't get your own glass. First, you won't know what is clean or not and you'll be demonstrating to him you're capable of doing simple things on your own. I know that the action of him serving you a drink might be misunderstood as you wanting to be waited on, but remember your goal, train him for you.

3. Now you have your glass, the question of what to do next comes up. Let him pour your drink. I know this might make you seem like a spoiled little bitch, but it is your first visit. He won't mind pouring it because he wants to impress you. If you do this on your fourth or fifth visits, then you ARE a spoiled little bitch, but for now, you're his guest. Once you've agreed to have a drink, listen to his small talk. There won't be much of it, but it will give you cues to his current level of training and enable you to gauge his level of development.

When you're offered a drink, the noun should be something like, "soda," "water," "juice," these words indicate he has had some training. Words like, "beer" or "shot," indicate he has had very little training or he figures you'd be easier if drunk.

4. Don't let him pour your drink. I know what I just said in the last step, but to train him properly, you should pour the first drink the first time you visit his apartment. Let him pour the second drink. If this seems confusing, welcome to our world. If he starts to pour your drink, let him. If he puts the glass down, you pour it. Don't rush anything. If you're not sure what to do, play it by ear. If you have no intension of ever visiting him again, do what you want. Skip this step and the next.

5. Don't get drunk. Don't get drunk. Because this is your first visit, the assessment visit if you will, don't get drunk. If you get drunk, then he'll think you're easy, he'll like that about you, but you won't. You can fake it. Women are good at faking it, so fake you're drunk. He won't notice. Remember, don't get drunk. I can't stress this enough. If you pass out on your first visit to his apartment, there's a great chance you will never see him again. He will not want to go out with a girl that drinks his liquor and doesn't do anything

in return except fall asleep. If you have to, when he's not looking, pour part of your drink into his glass. He won't notice and it will appear as if you're drinking enough for him. If you fall down drunk, it will make him think you're one of the guys. He doesn't want one of the guys right now. If he did, he would have invited them over instead of you. Realize he will drink two or three for every one of your drinks. Don't let him get too drunk either. The drunker he gets, the more he digresses and he will learn a lesson from you which you never want to teach; that it's okay for him to get drunk. It shouldn't be okay, so don't teach him it is by letting him get smashed on your first visit. It's okay to have a few drinks, it's okay to get tipsy, but falling-down drunk should not be okay. You're now asking, "How do I stop him from dinking?" I'm glad you asked. Here is how to keep him from getting drunk. You stop drinking after three drinks. Remember, he'll have two or three for your one, so by the time you have had three drinks, he's had six. If you slow down, he'll slow down. But if you have to be drunk to be with him, what the hell are you doing there in the first place? Do you want to drink with me? You want him sober enough to be civil, buzzed enough so he won't think you're judgmental and a bitch for not drinking with him. It's not that fine of a line. Six beers should do it. Once we've had several drinks, we're open to training. I know this is not a training visit, but never pass up an opportunity.

Let me give you an example of this. This is a true story. It took place before my wife and I were married. We had been dating for sometime so she took this opportunity to train me.

One night we decided to go out for dinner. I wanted to eat Mexican, but she wanted Italian. I already had a few drinks and thought we had decided on Mexican. We got in the car and I started driving. She kept making references to Italian. I was sober enough to be civil and buzzed enough to be open to suggestion. She started talking about the food, how good it would be and so on. Remember, the order of "Shit important to Men," food, TV, sex. I started getting hungry for Italian instead of Mexican. Before I knew it, we were pulling into the Italian restaurant parking lot. We went inside and I ordered food. I don't look at this as giving in, but more a great technique she used to train me to eat where she wanted to, when she wanted to. That training is till with me to this day. I don't have any idea why, but if we get into the car, we end up where she wants to eat. Fortunately for me, we agree on where we want to eat most times. Well, I think we agree. Come to think about it, I think I've been trained real well.

Chapter 4

The Phone is NOT Our Friend...

In the previous chapters, you've learned some basic things about men. You will need that foundation to build on. The remainder of the book assumes you've finished your mental assessment phase and decided to pursue a relationship. You've seen something in the man you've chosen, which leads you to believe he has potential. Only time will reveal if you've chosen wisely.

There comes a time in every relationship, whether or not it is a long term or short term thing; we must confront the phone test. Most men will fail this test the first few times it is attempted, but not for the reasons you might think. Most men want to pass this test, even though we find it a very hard step to take.

Men associate the phone with bill collectors. We don't like bill collectors. So when the phone rings, we associate the noise with bad things. Also, (I hope my mother skips this part), our mothers call us using that thing called a phone; we all know what that is like, nothing more on the topic of our mothers (sorry mom).

We fail this test not because we're afraid of commitment like most women think, but it's because we can't remember what the hell you look like. It's that simple. Remember we were drinking when we met you, slept with you, and promised to call. But do you remember if we used your name at any point during the encounter? We didn't.

We called you, "Baby" and "Honey" and other terms of endearment because we didn't remember your name.

What we do remember from that night is very simple. We remember we were with someone, that someone was fun, but we can't remember your face. We don't remember what clothes you had on, or off. We don't remember the clothes we wore, unless they're still on us, then we weren't with anyone and don't have to worry about calling anyone. Whatever the case may be, we don't remember much of that night. We won't remember you gave us your number until we do laundry and find the paper in one of our pockets. That is if we don't wash it by mistake, which happens very often. Which is another reason we don't call, we can't find your number.

So the phone test is an unfair test women put men through for no other reasons than to torture us. Instead of you giving us your number, you should take ours. Most men will still want your number, but if you want a return visit to the house of pleasure, you better take our number. And don't be afraid to use it. You might have to call us several times before we return the call, but that is because we don't remember what you look like. Once we remember, we'll call, or if you keep calling, we'll be dying to find out what you look like, so we'll call. Please remember to leave your name and a brief description of what we did together; this will help us remember you.

I have another real life experience I lived through which illustrates this point. I'd like to share it with you, (I have a lot of real life stories you'll read about in this book) but don't hold it against me.

This event also took place before I was married. I was at a bar with a few friends having some drinks. Actually, we were getting hammered. I saw a young lady sitting in the corner starring at me. Yes, she was looking only at me. I walked over to her and asked her name. I'm not sure why men do that, we know we're not going to remember and we really don't care, but we ask anyway. She told me her name, which I don't remember, and we started to talk. After about 30 minutes, she asked if was interested in going to a party she knew of going on by her house. Being the man that I am, I said, "Shit yeah." There I was, getting picked up by a woman, a female, a "hottie" and I didn't have to buy her a single drink. It felt good, no, it felt great.

We went to her place prior to going to the party. I don't remember how we got to her house, but I believe she drove. We went inside and had another drink before we walked down the street to where the party was. Yes, we "knocked one out" first, you have to have priorities. We also discussed whether I would spend the night at her house.

When we got to the party, I saw a few people I knew. Everyone was drinking, having a great time. The night seemed to last forever, well at least a two-hour stretch. Most people hate going to parties where they don't know anyone. For men, it is worse, unless there are plenty of women around. So it was a definite plus that I knew some people for a few reasons. First, I now had witnesses to verify I was with a woman. Yes, men require verification when they share the events of a night like that. Panties will usually suffice, but I had real live people to testify about this one.

By the time we had arrived at the party, I had already forgotten her name. Somehow I became very drunk. Not sure how that happened either. It was about this time I decided I should go back to her house and finish the night off with another ride on "Neil's fun machine." I found her at the party and mentioned my wishes. She said, "I don't have any more tickets left. Can I ride for free?" She had a great sense of humor. I told her we'd work something out.

As we made our way to the door, I saw a few people I wanted to say good bye to. She said she would go on ahead, leave the patio door unlocked and be waiting for me. Remember, I was really drunk. I'm not sure how long it took me to say goodbye to everyone, but I know it took longer than an hour.

I walked out of the house where the party was and started to walk to her house. It was only a few houses down the street. I got lost. Once I figured out I was walking the wrong direction, I turned around and made it to her house. I went in the backyard, opened the sliding glass door. It was unlocked just like she said it would be.

The house looked a bit different then I remembered it, but I was drunk. Sitting in the living room, I decided to turn on the stereo. She wasn't in the house and I thought she went back to the party to find me. So I sat there waiting for her to come back. There I was, sitting in her house, listening to the radio on low just waiting for her to show up.

I must have been waiting a long time because I fell asleep on the floor in front of the stereo. Sometime around seven am, I was awakened by a man kicking me lightly in the side. He kept saying, "Who are you?" and asking what I was doing in his house. I started thinking it was her father or boyfriend, maybe her husband. It never dawned on me I was in the wrong house.

That's right; I walked into someone else's house, turned on their stereo and fell asleep on their floor. I explained to him I was at the party down the street. He told me he remembered me from the party and knew the young lady I was with. Her house was the next house over. I have to admit he was pretty calm about the situation. He told me to sleep it off and lock up before I left.

To this day, I can't remember where the party was, what her name was, or who the guy was. I took a cab back to the bar, got my car and went home.

That story demonstrates men don't remember events as they're happening, let alone the next day. I know some men don't suffer from this, but those are the men who have been trained or had some training in the past. They have evolved. So don't think that because we didn't call, we're not interested. It's just we have a memory problem.

Look at the phone this way; we have a hard enough time participating in meaningful conversation while we're sitting in front of you, the phone does not make it any easier. It does offer us the opportunity to be naked while we're talking to you, but that is the only real plus.

The phone is a tool women use to test men. It's a tool men use to order pizza. If you met a guy in a bar, had sex with him, then gave him your number and expected him to call, you're expecting too much. If you didn't have sex with him, he'll call very soon. But, if you didn't have sex because of erectile dysfunction due to alcohol, he'll never call. He's too embarrassed.

There are hundreds of reasons why he won't call, but if he was interested and didn't call, it's because he can't remember your name or what you look like. Don't take it personally.

Now let's assume you have had a few dates with this guy. You've given him your number and you're waiting for him to call. Why? You've had a few dates, you can call him. It's okay for you take that step, but don't call him every day. People call that stalking, and it will push him away quicker than you can say "marriage."

You're in the first stages of training him, and just as in the previous chapter, you have to tread lightly with the phone test. Don't expect too much too soon.

The phone test might take you several months of repetitive suggestions to get him to call. In today's world, everyone has cell phones, so you might be able to accelerate the training a bit. This is because in the old days, most of us didn't have phones, we couldn't afford them. The phone bill ate into our beer money too much. We had to prioritize. Today everyone text's, surf's and tweets (I don't know what a tweet is, but I'm told it's cool).

There is also another important reason we might not call you. We're testing you. Correct, men think if the women we're with call us, then we're great in bed and you won't be able to live without us. That's the truth of it.

However, if you don't call, well, it won't really matter to us because we can't remember what you looked like and definitely don't remember your name. So we figure it's no great loss. But beware, we will talk to our friends and you will be portrayed as the "crazy bitch submitting to our every desire." After all, we were the best you ever had. We know it and you can't say anything to change our mind.

Here's a time-table for you to gauge not only our interest in you, but our memory of you.

If men call within one week, they're hooked. You can begin training at your convenience and treat us like a loyal dog. Every now and then you just have to give us a bone or two and maybe even a doggy treat. We will need plenty of reinforcement training, so a lot of bones would be better.

If we call between one to three weeks, then we're wondering if you still remember us, or we just remembered who you are. We've decided we want to get together again and are hoping you feel the same way.

If we call anytime after three weeks, one of a few things has happened. We lost your phone number and just found it. Believe me, this is very possibly the truth. Men aren't smart enough to lie about that one. It could be that we haven't had sex with anyone in a few weeks and know you're a better than fifty-fifty chance because at one point you were a willing partner.

Sex is the single most valuable tool a woman has. It will make men change Gods. It can make most men forget all their training and teachings since birth. This is another reason why we might not call, you made us forget. We remember the sex; we might not remember who it was with. But never use sex as a weapon. You already know what I mean, so no explanation is required.

If you never plan on seeing us again, don't bother telling us your name. We don't really care and it will make it very uncomfortable for both of us when we're done. You know, ten minutes later when we call you by another name.

I'm not telling you stop the one-night stand; just don't tell us your name. Also, we are scared of the story you're going to tell your friends. All women talk. So do men.

Here's our standard story if you decide you're not going to see us again. After we took you home, you became a psycho bitch and we can't be left alone in the same room as you again. This is code to all men, you have to bang her. She was freaky good.

However, if you do chose to have sex with us because of some impulsive behavioral tendenices, just bang the hell out of us and go on your merry way. This way, you can call us "Super Stud" and we don't have to call you at all.

If you are trying to build a relationship with us, please let us know in advance. We'll put your number in a safe place and actually write your name on it with a note to remind us of who you are. If we had a great time with you, we're going to call. If we didn't have a great time, please refer to the time table (earlier in the chapter) for when you can expect a call.

Any man who claims not to think like this, well, he's lying. At one point in our lives we have all thought exactly like this.

This may seem crass, but it's only meant to point out some basic reasons for some of the things we do, or don't.

If you are using the phone test to determine if he is "Mr. Right," you're using the wrong test. And for the record, Mr. Right doesn't exist. It becomes a matter of what you're willing to settle for. Lower the bar a bit and see what good men are out there.

Then again, you could always look at the phone test like this. If you woke up with a strange phone number in your pocket, would you call it? If you answered "yes" to that question, please let me know, I have a number you can call.

Chapter 5

This is My Apartment, You're just visiting...

This chapter is a bit long. It needs to be. The importance of the foundation you're trying to build is high. Besides, it will pay off if you're able to train him enough to be ready for marriage.

Now you've been dating sometime, things are going great, and it's time to take the next step; living together. The logical choice would be for the man to move into your apartment. It's nicer, cleaner, better organized and smells good. This will not happen. You're going to have to suck it up and move in with him.

Don't give up your apartment just yet. I know paying for a place you're not living in is hard to rationalize and digest, but it's a safety net you might need. I would wait a few months before completely committing to one home. Things change once that step is taken, and sometimes they don't change for the better. If you have no place to fall back on, you might feel pressured into compromising your goal of training your man. Keep your place for at least three months.

There is a certain amount of pride a man feels when "his" woman moves in with him. This pride is an essential part of his mental well-being. It is also a necessary element he must retain if you want to train him well. If you take it away, your man will not stay long, or I should say, you won't stay long. I know it sucks, but you have to move in with him, not the other way around. Don't worry, it's not that bad. In no time at all, you'll have his place looking great, smelling great and he'll be feeling great in the process. In other words, he'll never know what hit him.

Another important piece of this you should consider is his friends. They will come over. If they see the place cleaned up, it smells good, no dishes in the sink and frilly things on the couch; they will make fun of him. It will give them the impression he no longer has control. It will also make them slightly combative with you. After all, you're taking their friend away from them. In their minds, you're the reason little Jimmy can no longer come out and play. In guy talk, he's whipped. You must avoid this as it will only lead to tension between you and him, him and his friends, and you and his friends. You won't believe this, but you will lose in all those cases the first year you're living together. After that, you're on safer ground.

When a woman moves in with "Her" man, she automatically assumes she is in charge. While this is true, she cannot exploit it yet. There is an art form to letting your man think he is in charge while you pull the strings.

Don't start making rules for the home and immediately begin changing everything, including the décor (what little there is of it). This is the wrong way to go about transforming the apartment from the dog house it is into the castle you want it to become.

You have to remember your man already views his home as a castle. The only change he will accept is you moving in. He is not expecting you to replace his treasured items with foreign items such as a real couch, chair and TV stand. Well maybe not the TV stand. For all you know, he might have agreed to let you move in because of your TV stand.

In most men's apartments, there are four rooms, the kitchen, living room, bathroom and bedroom. Transforming each room has its own timetable and procedures. Transform one room before the other, and you could cause a meltdown. Transform a room too quickly, it could send your man into a coma. Each room has to be transformed in order, which we'll discuss, and on a timetable to prevent your man from taking more drugs than he must. Yes, he's taking drugs - or he wouldn't have agreed to let you move in. It doesn't matter whose idea the co-habitation was, you still need to respect his junk and yes, he will still need drugs the first few months.

Notice I left out the hallway in naming the rooms. This is because the hallway is a judgment call on your part. If your man accepts the changes we're going to discuss well, you can do the hall anytime after the kitchen. If on the other hand, your changes are rejected, you might want to wait on the hall until the pain has subsided.

In addition, each room has rules and those rules need to be changed accordingly and in conjunction with the visual changes. There are rules you can change fast and rules you'll need to ease in slowly. We'll cover the rules as we cover the room. To keep the transformation from disturbing him dramatically, don't replace too many things at once. Take it slow and steady.

Let's start with some basic, general rules of the apartment. These rules don't apply to any single room, but rather the entire home as a whole.

1. **You are a visitor**. Realize this sooner, rather than later. I know you're living together, but it is not "our home," it is "his home." This will change very quickly, but you have to give it the proper time to be absorbed. It should only take about two or three months. Coincidently, this is about the same amount of time you're still paying for your old apartment. Once you've completely moved all your stuff from your old place into his, then it becomes "ours" and ceases to be "his."

2. **You're not his Mother (or keeper)**. Don't expect he'll let you know everything he's doing or, when. Living together is new for him. When he lived with his parents, he had rules he swore would not apply to him once he moved out on his own. Don't start re-imposing those rules. The first few weeks,

he's going to do what he wants, when he wants. This too will change with time. Keep this in mind.

3. **If you want it clean, clean it**. Remember your first visit? Well, it will be your first visit every day for about three weeks. If you start nagging him to pick up after himself, you'll find out real soon why you kept your apartment. He'll clean a few things, but don't expect too much.

4. **Never talk while he's watching TV**. This is a biggie. You have something to say, save it for the commercial break. That is the best time to get his attention. But be prepared, once the sporting event or program he's watching is back on, you're going to lose his attention very fast. So say what you have to say, and say it quickly.

5. **Don't plan social events**. This means no parties to welcome you into the home. It also means you can't invite your friends over without mentioning it to him first. I'm not saying you need his permission, but just a little comment like, "My friend Sue is coming over tomorrow, we're going to make out. Just thought I'd let you know." Trust me on this; he'll have no issues if you put it that way, but if he comes home and finds a bunch of your friends in his apartment, he'll be pissed.

6. **You cannot kick anyone out of his place.** His friends, his dog, his dead goldfish floating in the

bowl, they are all off limits to you for now. You can't say, "I don't want him here." This won't fly in his home. Give it time and eventually you'll be able to kick him out, but for now, live with the dead goldfish. After all, his mother bought it for him and he doesn't know how to tell her it's been dead since the fourth day he got it. Nobody told him to feed it goldfish food, not Frosted Flakes. It's not his fault.

7. **Time is irrelevant**. After a few days, he's not going to be home until well after 5am. He's not going to call you to let you know he'll be out all night, so get over it, and I mean real fast. Let it go unless you want a real argument on your hands. I'm telling you now, don't stay awake for him. If you do, you're a fool. He won't call and he won't apologize for it (refer to rule #2; you can also refer to Chapter Four). You have to remember he is not accustomed to living with anyone, so your presence in his apartment is still a novelty. It won't matter if you asked him to call, it won't happen for at least four months and he will still forget from time to time. Don't get mad and have the locks changed, don't put his stuff on the porch. Get over it!

If you chose to make a big deal of now, here's what you're in for: He's been out drinking all night, which means he's drunk. If you lock the door, he'll break a window to get in and throw your stuff out. Remember, the first few months, in his mind you're a visitor.

Time for a training lesson:

If you insist on broaching the subject within the first hours of your breaking Rule 7, here's how to do it. Do not be accusatory, be concerned. Questions like, "Why didn't you call?" don't get answered the way you want and so will only make you angrier. Another question you shouldn't ask is, "Where have you been?" That question always comes out the wrong way. It demonstrates a lack of trust and right now, you need the trust if you're going to mold him correctly. After you've been together for years, yell and scream all you want, but for now, it's still only the first few weeks you've been living together.

Your best bet is concern. Questions like, "Are you alright?" will show your concern. Statements of concern always get a better response, such as, "I stayed up worrying about you. I thought you might have been in an accident." If you tried his cell phone and there was no answer, you can always add, "I tried your cell, but nobody answered. I wanted to let you know I was going to bed." Don't use that line if you didn't try his cell. He'd know you were bullshitting him. But, if you did call his cell, you've just given him the false security he needs to have when you lower the hammer on him.

The hammer is simple... it's guilt. It's easy to make him feel guilty. Just like you would talk in a strict voice to a dog when the dog poops on your bed, you can do the same thing to your man. Use a stern, authoritative voice and say the concern statement. Look at his face after that, note his expression and give him a hug. Shit, girl - now you own him.

For now, that should cover the general rules. Remember, all those rules will change in time. You just have to allow them to progress according to the natural order of the galaxy. Now let's move to the visual parts of transforming your dungeon into your palace.

The first room to transform should be the bedroom. The bedroom is not used at all by his friends, so he won't feel he has to hide your feminine touch from them. You spend about a third of your time in there, but most of that is really sleeping. It is also a great place to test his comfort level of change prior to infesting the rest of the home (yes, I said infesting).

You'll notice the clothes are lying on the floor, the bed is not made and most of the drawers in his dresser (if he owns a dresser), are open with things hanging out. Don't panic. It will only take you about three weeks to get it in order.

Let's deal with the clothes on the floor first. If you look in the closet, you'll see the hamper. Nothing should be in it. Pull it out and place it in the room right in front of him. Every time he walks into the room, he will see the hamper. He'll probably ask what it's doing in the middle of the room; just let him know that you're trying to make his life a bit easier. Since he can't put his clothes in the hamper located in the closet, you've decided it would be better for him if the hamper was in the middle of the room, on his side of the bed.

Don't make the mistake of thinking he'll care if the hamper is next to his side of the bed or in the middle of the room. He won't, and you're betting he won't. After a few days of him dropping his clothes in the hamper, move it. That's right, move it closer to the closet by about two feet. He won't notice the move and continue to put his clothes in the hamper.

After another few days, move it again, just a bit closer to the closet. Remember not to move it too close too soon. Subtle changes in distance will not be noticed.

Once you have the hamper just outside the closet door, wait a few days and put it in the closet. Don't shut the closet door. This will only confuse him. He'll start putting his clothes on the floor and you'll have to start all over. Leave the closet door open enough so he can see the hamper in the closet. He'll start putting the clothes in there and think nothing of it.

After a few more days, ask him to close the closet door when he's done in it. Ask nicely, but remember to use your little girl voice. You know what I'm talking about so don't pretend you don't.

Open the closet door before he gets home from work or any time prior to you guys getting ready for bed. Again, after he's put his clothes in the hamper, ask him to close the door. You're going to have to do this for about a week.

Once he completes a week of closing the door, reverse it. You start closing the closet door and have him open it when he needs to put his clothes in the hamper. He'll be a bit confused at first. He won't see the hamper (out of sight, out of mind), so you might have to remind him it's in the closet.

He'll start opening the door, putting his clothes in the hamper, and then, yes, closing the door. No more clothes on the floor, everything in the hamper and the closet door is closed. Congratulations, you've just trained him and he has no idea it was done.

This method is similar to the "news-paper" method used when training a dog to only go on the paper. Every week you remove some of the paper and the area the dog can soil gets smaller and smaller. Same concept for the hamper.

At the same time you're training him to use the hamper; you can work in a little training on making the bed. But you have to wait until the hamper is just outside the closet door to start this task.

First, start by asking him to help you pull the covers over the bed. It doesn't have to be made nice, just so the covers hide the sheets. DO NOT put a comforter on the bed unless he already has one. You know - that fluffy thing that goes over the actual covers, serves no purpose but to make the bed look nice and gives most men the chills when we see it. We get the chills because we don't know what a comforter is for. We have no idea how to act. If you notice, when we go into a hotel room, the first thing we do is pull the comforter off and throw it on the floor. It's equivalent to the same reaction you would have if you found a dead rat, except we don't scream as loud.

After about a week of him helping you semi-make the bed, you can introduce the neatness of the concept. Pull the covers over the sheets, make them look neat and nice, no wrinkles. Putting the pillows under the covers, you know, however you like the bed to be made. But still without the comforter, we'll get to that in a bit. You can do the comforter yourself.

One morning, pretend you're running late for work. Ask him to make the bed before he leaves. If he always leaves for work before you, make up a reason you have to leave earlier than usual. You have to get him to do it on his own. He's going to mess it up the first time he flies' solo on this. The covers won't be perfect, I'm not sure they'll even be straight, but they'll be on the bed.

Now might be a good time to hang a picture in the hallway.

When you get home, check out the job he did on the bed. Whether it looks good or bad, thank him for doing it. You can pull this trick about three times a week for about three weeks. Then you get to let him fly on his own. You're going to have to remind him now and then about the clothes and bed, just remember that.

Okay, yes, now is the time you can introduce the "serves no purpose whatsoever" comforter. You're going to have to put it on the first few times by yourself. Let him see it and become comfortable with it. Let him touch it so he can realize it's not going to bite and it won't hurt him. He has to know the comforter is a friend.

Once he gets accustomed to seeing it on the bed, it's just a simple reminder to him to make sure he puts the comforter on the bed once it's made. You're not going to get out of making the bed entirely, you're still going to have to help him every so often, or he will start to feel like your slave.

Remember, just as all dogs like a bone after being good, so do men. You're going to have to give him a bone, better make it two. The reward reinforces the lesson.

Now is a good time to hang something on the wall in the hallway.

Here comes the hardest part of training him to make the bed: putting the f@#king stuffed animals on the bed. We don't know where each animal goes, so don't expect us to. Understand in some minds of men, seeing a stuffed animal on the bed reminds us of our sister's room when we were growing up. We don't want to sleep with our sister, well, most of us don't. If we don't have a sister, it can remind us of our mothers. In either case, we are not comfortable with thinking of female relatives in conjunction with beds.

Don't get me wrong, you can train him to accept stuffed animals as equals in the room, but you're going to pay for it. If you do it correctly, the animals will become erotic additions. Here's how:

Put on your sexiest night gown, pajamas or whatever you sleep in. If you sleep in a night-gown that reminds us of grandma, change. That is not sexy. Call to him while lying on the bed. If he's not eating or watching TV, he'll be right there. Act seductive and flirt, you might want to talk dirty to him if you're into that. Once he is on the bed, pull out one of the stuffed animals and start playing. We may be dense, but we're not that dense. We know what is coming next and we'll love the animal like we've never loved anything or anyone before. That little fury f@#ker will never know what hit it.

Now is a good time for a bone. We made a great and generous concession accepting that animal into our bed, and now it's time for you to pay up.

Go ahead and hang something on the wall in the hallway at this point. Heck, you can hang two things on the wall in the hallway after that. I need a cigarette. Let's move on.

If your bathroom is connected to the bedroom and is not a standalone room, you're going to have to start there next. If it's a standalone room you access from the hall, you might want to wait a week or so before tackling it.

Either way, you're going to have to clean it the first time yourself. Put on your wetsuit, your water-proof clothes, wrap yourself in plastic, do whatever you need to do so you're able to walk in without needing a tetanus shot or antibiotics. You might still need both, but the infection risk is minimized tremendously by taking appropriate precautions. Let's assume the bathroom is connected to the bedroom.

While you're training him to put his clothes in the hamper and to make the bed, you can start to add very subtle changes to the bathroom. The only change which is not subtle at all is the initial cleaning. Don't be afraid. If he senses fear, you won't get him to participate in the first cleaning. You probably won't get him to help anyway, but fear will seal the deal and you'll be on your own.

On second thought, don't ask him to help, just dive in and get it done. Quit complaining and just clean the thing. This will put you in a good place. Not only will you feel good that the bathroom is usable, but it's a great starting point for him to see what it looks like clean. Remember, the only other time he has seen his bathroom clean was the day he moved in.

There's going to be hair and stains everywhere. Don't point to a stain and ask, "What is that?" just hold your breath and start cleaning.

An important note here; put everything back where you found it. Don't move his shaving cream to another place; don't throw out the bar of soap unless you're going to replace it with a new one. Don't throw out anything yet.

You can have some of your items on the counter, but do not dominate the space. There will be time for that later.

This is just the first cleaning of many to come. But while we're on the subject of your stuff, you can make room without his permission for one drawer and about one square foot of counter space. You may not put any more than four items in the shower. I know this will be hard for you. Trust me, you'll manage. I have one bottle of shampoo and one bottle of body wash. My wife has half the beauty isle from Wal-Mart in our shower. Don't get me started on this. So, four items only, for now.

Once you've cleaned the bathroom to your liking, you can start training him to keep it that way. The first time he goes in the bathroom after the cleaning, he's going to come out and you're going to hear, "Shit, look at that." He's then going to say, "Did you clean the bathroom?" I know why he's going to ask, and now I'll tell you why. We know we didn't clean it, but believe it or not, it never enters our mind that you might have. We think a little bathroom fairy came in, waved her little magic wand, and everything became clean. I kid you not, we really do think this. Your answer should be along the lines of, "I just straightened up a bit because I needed a little space." The moment you say little space, he's going to run back into the bathroom and check to make sure the bar of soap with the hair on it is still there.

For now, be content knowing that you've cleaned up; it won't be that hard for him to help in keeping it clean. It won't take much training, because he likes the bathroom clean, he just doesn't like to clean it. Just keep reminding him to rinse out the sink, and take out the trash and he should be fine.

I can't help with the toilet seat being up or down. Twenty one years and counting of marriage, and I still can't remember if it goes up after I've sat on it, or down, or down after I put it up. Shit, it's just too confusing for me. I'll tell you the same thing I tell my wife, "look before you sit."

You can apply the same lessons for the bathroom (if it's not connected to the bedroom), but you'll have to wait a week or so. If you have two bathrooms, it will take double the time to train him. But you can't do both bathrooms simultaneously. It will confuse him and make your job harder. One at a time and about one week apart should be good.

Hang something else on the hallway wall.

About six weeks should have passed by now. You should take a week off from the transformation process. This will allow the changes to settle within his brain and won't upset the delicate ecological balance he's cultivated in his home. It will also give you a break. Even the trainer needs some time off. Give him a bone and you take a break.

Your third room should be the kitchen. His friends only go in there to get beer from the refrigerator and chips from the cupboard, if the snacks are not already on the table or stuffed in the cushions of the couch. A change in the kitchen won't make that big of an impact on him or his friends, but it will start the mental conditioning process required to change the main room of the apartment, the living room.

Men must learn not all dishes are disposable. Paper plates and paper cups in the trash, all others go in the sink. To teach us this, start by just asking us to put everything in the sink. Yes, paper and all. After a week or so, once the sink is full, invite us into the kitchen. Wear something sexy, but not dressed-up sexy, more along the lines of slutty sexy.

You're about to turn doing the dishes into foreplay. You have to be careful with this, if you do it too often, every time he does dishes he's going to want a reward, you know, another bone.

Mention that you thought it would be fun to do the dishes together. Make sure you use soap and gently caress his hands as you grab a dish, encourage him to be a bit playful. Maybe splash him a little. The objective is to get your man to associate the dishes with a good thing in his life. It's very scientific; studies have been done using animals and positive encouragement and reinforcement. If it works with dogs, it will work with men.

Once he feels comfortable doing the dishes, he'll have no issues in the future. Getting him to put them in the dishwasher is a bit tricky. This is because we don't understand why you have to wash the dishes first, and then put them in the dishwasher to get washed. It seems a waste for us to do both. Don't try to explain it, it won't help. My wife says the dishes go in the dishwasher, and that's where I have my sons put them.

To get your man to put the dishes in the dishwasher just tell him that is where they go to dry. By now, you have more influence on him and some of what you say will be listened to without question.

To get him to put the dishes away after they've been run through the dishwasher is a bit harder. The dishwasher door is closed and we won't remember the last time it was ran. Remember the "out of sight" adage. Those little magnets you put on the door that reads, "Clean" on one side and "Dirty" on the other won't help either, so don't try it.

The best way for you to teach us to put the dishes away, is to ask for something in the dishwasher. When he opens it to get your request, he'll ask if they are clean. Just respond with a "yes" and then ask if he'll put them away since he's standing there. You might want to help him the first few times or most of the dishes are going to end up in one cabinet. They won't be separated by size and type. The silverware drawer will be a mess. After a few times helping him, leave him alone and let him go. Remember to reward him for his achievement. Another bone will work well.

For the trash, use the same technique as you did for the dirty clothes on the floor. Pull the trash can out from under the sink, and let it be seen. Move it every so often towards the sink and in no time you'll have it back under the sink and he'll be throwing trash in it. To remind him where the trash can has been moved to, just a note on the door that reads, "trash" will work. I know it sounds foolish, but it does work. If you have a trash compactor, you've hit the jackpot. Men love toys, and the trash compacter is a great toy. Just tell him to push the compact button after he puts the trash in.

Here's some bad news about the kitchen: The oven is all yours. He'll clean the stove top, but never expect him to do the inside of the over. In twenty years of marriage, I've cleaned the inside of our oven once. I sprayed the entire can of oven cleaner into it, let it sit for a few hours (following the directions, okay, not really) and nothing happened. I still had to scrub it. So from that point on, I decided I would rather replace the oven before I ever cleaned it again.

The last room to have a make-over will be the living room. I know what you're thinking, "Why can't it be the first room?" The answer is simple. It's the first room everyone sees when they first enter the apartment and therefore is the last room you can change.

The living room is the first room which reveals change to the world. That is why changing the living room first will send your man into cardiac arrest. He'll never make it past the threshold if that is the first room transformed. That is why you need to start at the very back of the apartment and work your way forward. You have to give him time to digest the changes gradually and become comfortable with them over time.

Also, the living room is the room you want to look the nicest, to have the highest degree of femininity (dam that word was hard to type) and it's one of the hardest rooms to transform without making your man feel emasculated.

I presume you have nice furniture of your own, and it's still in your old apartment. Now is the time for all good men to rise to the occasion, that's right, you're moving out of your old place. This is another reason why I warned you not to move out of your old place too soon. You didn't have any place to move your stuff to. Now you may fully take over and start calling his apartment "ours" instead of "his," that is, once all your stuff is moved in.

Let's start with the carpet. It's going to need a deep cleaning. You may think it looks clean now, but once you move the couch, you're going to find out the dark blue carpet is really light blue. You don't want to move anything in until you move everything out and clean the carpet. A good way for you to handle this change will be for you to invite him back to your old place and have him help you move some clothes.

Once you're at your old place, mention how good your couch will look inside his apartment. Chances are he'll agree. Right then and there make plans for the weekend to move it. Do this before he has a chance to realize what just happened. Make him commit to the move, and make sure to schedule it is as soon as possible. Offer to pay for the U-Haul pickup truck if you need one. Offer to buy his buddies a case of beer so they'll help. You're going to need help, because you're not just moving the couch on Saturday, you're moving everything. But don't tell him yet.

Before the weekend, you're going to want to rent a carpet cleaner and proceed with steam cleaning the living room. Be careful not to clean too far into the hallway, or you'll find yourself having to clean that too, then the bedroom and before you know it, you've just spent ten hours cleaning.

When the weekend comes, get the truck and go with your man to your old place to meet his buddies. You have to be there. Don't just throw him the keys. It won't turn out well if you do that. Go with him and get ready to drop the great news on him. Say, "You know, since we have the truck, we might as well move more of this stuff." He'll think for a minute before answering, but he's not thinking about agreeing with you, he's wondering if there's enough beer to bribe his buddies. Offer to get more beer and pizza and its moving day!

Make sure you grab your refrigerator. If you noticed, when we covered cleaning the kitchen, I didn't mention it. That's because you don't need to clean it, you're going to replace it with yours.

When you get back to your (notice I said your, not his) new apartment, you can start throwing out everything in the living room with one exception. I don't care how many bones you give him; you're not getting rid of the reclining chair. I know it has holes; it's covered by a blanket with unidentifiable stains and is most likely stuck in the open position. You're not getting rid of it unless you're prepared to buy him a new one.

While we're on that subject, when you do buy a new chair, it will serve you well to remember it's his chair, not yours. He gets to pick out the color, the style, the size and yes, he gets the chair with the beer holder built in.

Now that you're back unloading the truck, I would recommend moving the refrigerator first. Get it plugged in and stocked up right away. Your man and his buddies are going to be hungry and thirsty. You'll get them to work more if you offer to pay for more pizza and more beer. But wait until the truck is empty. This is because you can now send them back to your old place to get more stuff, and inform them that the pizza and beer will be waiting for them when they return. Now you can send him alone while you stay and start arranging stuff.

Depending on how much furniture you have, you might need to move more the next day. Getting his buddies to help two days in a row will be hard, but not impossible. So be nice and let them act like men and move your stuff. It's advisable to give your man a bone after he moves everything, but not his buddies, unless you're into that sort of thing, than by all means let me know when you're moving again, I'll help.

Once you start putting everything in the living room, the arrangement of the furniture shouldn't be hard. Most likely the room isn't large enough to offer many options for placement. Have the guys place the items in the spot you want, so know where you want everything. The previous few months you should have been planning this out so when moving day came, you knew exactly where each piece of furniture would go. Don't keep changing your mind. I hate when my wife asks me to hang a picture, but has no idea where she wants it. I have to stand there, holding the thing up in millions of locations on the wall separated only by a few millimeters before she finally says, "That's it. Hang it there." If you do that, you're going to be hanging and moving things yourself. Remember I've been trained. It took my wife years to get me to participate in her insanity.

Like I said, you should know where you want the stuff. After everything is placed where you want it or close, tell your man to go out and do something with his friends. This gives you an opportunity to clean up a bit, rearrange things a bit and gives him an opportunity to unwind after moving. If you need his friends to help the next day, you're going to have to let him go out and play a bit. Remember, you don't want the guys hanging out because you need to transform the room a bit.

Once he's gone, do your stuff. Make magic in the room, but no flowery throw pillows on the couch just yet. Drink coasters are acceptable, he won't use them, but they are a nice accent to the room. Pillows on the couch are okay, but nothing to feminine, not yet. Again, you have to give him time to adjust to the change.

There is never a good time to add the flowery throw pillows. I suggest giving it a few weeks, and then spring it on him.

Hang something in the hall.

Chapter 6

I thought your Dad liked me...

One of the hardest meetings a man will face in life is meeting your parents. Your father is the one person all men try to win over first, ever though everyone knows it's your mother who runs things. If we can win over your father first, your mother will come around easier.

One reason we try a run at your father first and ignore your mother is simple; we can take your mother. She's old, slow, and runs like a girl. Your father on the other hand, well, in addition to his preparation for this since the day you were born, he knows how to shoot. We really don't need him mad at us. You are his little girl, and we're the guy who's looking for permission to do to you the same thing he has been doing to your mother for years........(I know what you're thinking)......I'm talking about taking care of your needs and giving you companionship during good times and bad times (you were thinking of something else, I know).

Here is how the first meeting will most likely play out. You've been together for about six months: it's time to meet the parents. You mention the upcoming holiday and think it would be a great time for you to introduce him at the family gathering. The look on his face will tell it all. He is scared beyond all belief. Incidentally, this will be the same look you'll get if you bring up marriage or having children the first year you're together. It could also be the same look as when he saw those stuffed animals on his bed.

He will give you some grief about the meeting, but you'll win in the end. Just remember not to order him, just keep saying it's important to you. You're going to have to remind him several times the week before and the night before.

The day has come. He's dressed inappropriately for the occasion - you should've expected it. His T-Shirt reads, "Bad to The Bone," and the jeans might have a hole or two in them. He's trying to look tough for your father, and to project the image that he can take care of you. You can ditch the shirt, but let him keep the jeans on. You can also suggest he put on jeans without holes, but if you're going to be playing any kind of sports (like most family picnics) ask him to bring a pair of jeans he can change into for the events. You can make minor adjustments to his wardrobe, but be careful not to completely remake him; he needs to be a bit comfortable for this meeting.

A family gathering is also a good place for the first meeting, even though it's the most uncomfortable place for him. It's good for him to get used to it if you have a large family. Also, you'll be able to observe him as he interacts with other family members. Once he bonds with other males in your family, he'll be fine. You'll know he bonded with them because you'll see all of them acting like children.

You arrive at the designated location. Your man walks up to your father to shake his hand. From the moment your father and man saw each other; they have been sizing each other up. They are after all both men.

Your father is trying to gauge whether or not he can kick your man's ass if need be and your man is running the exact same estimate on your father. They each size up the other and visualize what the fight would look like. Your father's vision is much more graphic and ends with your man in little pieces buried in the backyard. Your man's vision is one of restraint. He pictures himself trying to keep from killing your father; he thinks your father is old and weak.

You can see the dilemma they both face. It will take a few moments for them to play out the scenario in their head before they'll be ready for the first hand shake.

The first hand shake is critical to both. Your father will always carry with him the first thoughts of this hand shake, whether or not your man's hand shake was firm, tough, gentle, weak or just girly. Instruct your man to be firm but not strong. This will relax your father.

Once they have moved past this initial silent test, the fun really begins. Watch your man, he's going to transform before your eyes. Don't say anything to him. If you have to say something, wait until you guys are in the car going home. Don't be that girl who calls her man out in front of the crowd just to make a point. Wait and you'll get a much better response when you're alone with him. You should be aware of this: you are going to change also. Your mannerisms will be different and he'll notice it. So be careful where you throw that stone, you know, the proverbial glass house and all.

It's important to us, as men, to win over your father. Your mother is also important, but we have to get your father in our pocket first or at least we need to think we have him in our pocket.

We know we need to win over your mother, but once we have your father, he'll inadvertently help with your mother. He'll make comments like, "he's a good kid, give him a chance." If your father has no opinion, we're screwed. He can't be on the fence when it comes to us. For your mother, we can kick her ass if we had to, so she can be on the fence for now.

During the "parents meeting," we're going to determine how much enthusiasm your father has in getting you married off. If he seems too eager to get rid of you, we're going to think one of two things.

First, we're going to think you might be stupid, or at least he thinks you might be too stupid to get married and you'll be an old maid and never be married. Yes, we're going to think this, but we'll dismiss it pretty quick, unless your father brings up a past boyfriend. Then, we're back on the stupid thing. We're also going to think there is something wrong with you that you haven't told us. You won't believe half the stuff we'll be thinking if your father is eager to get rid of you.

The second major thing we think is that your father is an ass. How could any father be so willing to give up his little daughter to some guy? Especially since he knows what your man is going to do to you in the bed room. You remember the stuffed animal experience, don't you?

But then we figure that you probably wouldn't have introduced him to us in the first place.

Here's a good place for another real story.

I knew a young girl who was being given away on her wedding by her father. No, I really mean "given away." She was one of those fortunate few who get to go through life oblivious to reality. She was a real ding-bat, but a very kind person. The guy she was marrying was actually paid by her father to marry her. No shit, he gave my buddy over ten thousand dollars to marry his daughter and promised to buy them a house. To my buddy, this was the perfect girl, daddy's rich, she's stupid and he can do what he wants and not have to worry about anything. For the record, he did what he wanted, when he wanted, and after a few years, her father cut him off and forced a divorce. My former buddy was a real ass.

Once your father accepts us into his fold, a great burden is lifted from us. We're one of the gang, the bunch, the "Wolf Pack." I know it sounds funny, but that doesn't make it any less true. We now have the permission we needed to call you "ours." It gives men a great sense of pride to have the blessings of their girlfriend's father.

When it comes to your mother, well, she's a mystery to us. One moment we think she worships the ground we walk on (like you do), the next, we're afraid to turn our back on her unless we want a knife sticking out of it. Your mother is a hard read, maybe that's because women, in general, are mysterious by nature.

My father-in-law was a great guy. After he passed away, it was devastating to my wife and believe it or not, to me also. I had a great affection for him and we got along great. We had a running joke for years. At the beginning of each year, he would give me twenty dollars to keep his daughter. It started with a comment on our wedding day I made to him. I said, "In order for me to keep her, I'll need twenty dollars every year." When he gave it to me in a card with an inscription which read, "Year One," I was floored. I thought, this is a guy with a sense of humor. He and I got along great from that point forward and, yes, I got twenty dollars from him every year until he died.

My wife's mother was just the opposite. She and I have never really hit it off. When my father-in-law was alive, she and I got along pretty well. Once he died, it all went to shit. Not sure why, but to this day, we still only tolerate each other.

That is why I say we need to win your father over first, as long as he's around, he'll be able to keep your mother in check. I still miss my father-in-law.

When you introduce your man to your parents, you should do everything you can to help him make a real impression, notice I didn't say a good impression. That is because your mother will see right through it, and your father will not be impressed. Maybe that's why I got along so well with him and not her, I was real.

After the first meeting and you're on your way home, your man is going to make some very retarded observations. He'll say things like, "Your dad and mom are cool, I think your dad really liked me." Or "I made a real good impression on them, I had them eating out of my hand." Your man is talking out of his butt and he knows it. I know he's trying to convince himself everything went great. It never goes great the first time. It only goes well at best. If he was able to walk away without getting punched by your father, it went well, not great. But you should lie to him in either case. Make him feel he did fantastic. Never tell him what your mother actually said, just leave it at "she liked you." He'll find out soon enough if it went bad.

You'll have to reward him with another bone, but you also get to hang something else on the hallway wall. It's a fair trade off.

Chapter 7

I'm not paying to have that Fixed…
(I can do it)

This chapter is going to be fun to write.

Most men are not dumb. Contrary to what most women think - what you call dumb, we call pride. Pride gets in the way all the time. You'll see us doing something which you would immediately consider dumb, you are confusing intelligence with pride. Don't make the mistake of thinking because we're standing in a puddle of water working on electricity that we have little to no intelligence, well, in that case it might be true, but there is a reason for everything we do, and most of the time it's pride.

Most men would rather die than call a trained professional to repair something we know we can fix. Again, it's pride. You know we're not going to fix it, we know we're not going to fix it, but that doesn't mean we won't spend twice as much time and money trying to fix it ourselves before paying someone else to do it.

When the toilet gets backed up, we use the plunger. Only when the plunger gets stuck do we call the plumber.

Let's pretend for a moment. Your man is outside, mowing the lawn. He's using a motorized lawn motor with a half horse power engine. It stops working. Engines and moving parts are a man's favorite thing to work on. Unless we're trained to repair small internal combustible engines, we're screwed. They're not hard to repair, but most men don't have the proper tools, which makes the repair process very difficult.

Real life story time again.

When I was sixteen years old, the engine in my truck froze up. I didn't have the money to buy a new engine, nor did I have the money to pay someone to repair it. I went to the library, borrowed the Chilton's Guide (the authoritative manual all mechanics use) for my particular truck and began to rebuild the engine with the help of a few friends.

I will admit we were very stoned when we started (it was the '70s) and throughout the entire process. I rented a cherry picker (engine lift) and bought the tools I didn't already own or couldn't borrow.

When we finished, which was about two days later, all of us felt a tremendous amount of pride. We just rebuilt a truck engine. Did I forget to mention that I had parts left over?

Well, I had a few small, non descriptive parts left over. Before I started up the truck, we sat around debating whether or not we should fire the bad boy up and just see what happens.

The consensus was to go for it. You may think my friends had no vested interest in my truck running, but you'd be wrong. This was the '70s, if you owned your own vehicle or had a best friend with one, you were cool. So my friends had in some ways a greater interest than I did in my truck running. Did I mention we were stone during this debate? We were.

I jumped in the truck and fired it up. Ran like the day it came off the factory floor. I didn't drive it for about an hour, I wanted to let it run for a while just in case. After we drove it, we came to the conclusion those extra parts were not needed. I was right.

Back then, most manufactures included extra parts just in case you lost one. I didn't know this, neither did my friends. It wasn't until a few weeks later that we found that out from another friend.

I learned from that experience I could fix anything. I believe this is how most men come to the realization they are, wait for it…"Repair Gods of All Things." This false sense of security seems to get men into more trouble fixing things than all other influences combined. My wife is very fond of saying, "I'll get the number for the guy to fix it so when you're done fixing it we can call and get an appointment."

Yes, we've all seen the repair shows that feature "How To" topics, and cool new tools we'll never need or use but must have. Here's where I tell you to install parental controls on his TV (yes, it's still his for now) so he can't watch those shows. It will only cost him, and you, more money and heartache than is necessary and what is already in store for you.

These shows feed our desire to use toys. Tools are toys for most men. The more intricate the tool looks - the less we understand what it does, the more we need it.

When the kitchen sink gets clogged, you'll see the tools come out and the testosterone flow like water. Same holds true for anything that breaks in the house, the car, the world. We will fix it.

Men will fix everything except what you ask us to fix. We don't change light bulbs when you want, we won't replace the toilet paper roll (that is not fixing anything), and we don't know what to do with the toilet seat (previously discussed).

If it doesn't require a tool, then it's not considered "fixing" at all. You must have tools and the opportunity to get messy for men to agree it can be called "fixing something."

When a man goes to the bathroom, if the light bulb is burned out, we'll go with the door open. We won't change the bulb because it's the wrong time to do that. We're in there to read and, well, other things, but one of them is definitely not changing the light bulb. If we remember after we're done with our business, we might change the light bulb.

If you want the light bulb changed, you have to ask when we're not on our way in there. Here's how to get the bulb changed:

Tell your man dinner is ready. Hand him the light bulb and ask him, do not demand, but ask him to change the bulb in the bathroom before he washes his hands for dinner. He'll have the bulb in his hands, he'll associate the bulb with the darkness in the bathroom, and presto, he'll change the bulb, wash his hands and you'll have passed another milestone on your path to training him. Association works well. After dinner, if the bulb got changed, go into the bathroom and give him a bone. Again, we're back to association.

Be careful, he might just run around the house changing every bulb, whether or not they need changing. He really likes those bones.

I'll admit, men don't always use the correct tool for the correct job, but when a hammer and duct tape will work, why would we use anything else?

Believe it or not, men have feelings. Well, it's all feelings and emotions wrapped into one, but it's our feeling. There is no single word to describe that one feeling, just know it's there and it covers the spectrum.

Yes, you can hurt our single feeling. Not giving us credit where credit is due, or not recognizing effort where effort was put forth, the lack of these actions will bruise our ego and hurt our feeling.

Most men will not admit you bruised our egos or hurt our feeling. But it will show in our actions. Please make an effort to identify this and correct yourself by giving us a compliment. Oh shit, I used the "C" word. That's right; you have to compliment him every now and then.

Just giving us a bone will not always work, but please don't stop, you have to also support and give encouragement. Even when you disagree, you have let him try. If he fails, don't say, "I told you so," this is not encouragement - it's just not. Saying something more like, "It was a great try; I was hoping you would be able to do it." This type of encouragement will do and you wouldn't have hurt his single feeling.

Look at it this way, we want to fix everything first. We want to show our woman we do just as good of a job as the next guy. Set aside your thoughts that it is going to take three days longer than necessary and cost much more. The job will get done and that is the only thing which should matter. If the job is completely messed up, he'll know it and have you call the professional. Please wait for him to give the signal it's time to bring in a trained professional. Here's how you'll know it time;

It will sound like this, "Shit, I can't fix this thing. Maybe we should just buy a new one?" Or "I've never seen this do that before." These are your cues to suggest you guys call someone. He's going to resist with something like this, "Honey, I'm telling you it is gone, dead, beyond repair. We just need to get a new one." If it is something you need replaced, then by all means, let him believe it's nothing more than a paper weight now and go buy another. But if we're talking about something like the TV, refrigerator, and microwave over or the powered lawn mower, you might want to take it to a repair shop and see what they say.

Men love toys, as I said before. We love to build them, race them, crash them and then fix them. Sometimes we will take a perfectly fine working item, tear it apart and rebuild it just because we can. We shouldn't do this, but we must, its part of our genetic makeup and engrained in our DNA. We have no choice, we must fix things.

There is a unique "Oneness" we feel when we're in the zone fixing things or building them. When we're done, we want to show them off to the world. We're looking for acceptance into the "Cool Men's" club. The plain "Men's Club" is a rite of passage into the "Cool Men's" club. But once we've achieved "Cool" status, only another member can request you be removed. From that point on, everything you fix or build is labeled, "Made by a Cool Man" for all eternity.

At some point in every man's life he must try to enter this club. From childhood fathers teach their sons about the club, show them how to fix things which aren't broken yet, go beyond when fixing something and how to show it off to the world. WE ARE MEN. Wow, that was a great paragraph for me, was it good for you too? I need a cigarette.

Hang something on the wall, I'm feeling good.

When men are involved with a woman, they truly only have two thoughts going through their heads at any single point, one is how do I please my woman. Most time this thought will involve sex or building something. The second thought is how I can make that better, again, this thought also involves sex or building something. We don't think about food because it's a given you're going to feed us.

When your man builds you a bookshelf, you don't say, "It took you two weeks to build that!" No, you should say, "Oh, you built me a bookshelf. How nice of you. I know just where it is going to go." We need that, we crave that type of encouragement.

If every time you tell your man to call someone to come in a fix what is broke, you're really telling him you have no faith in his ability. This hurts us and will lead us to never calling a professional, if for no other reason than pride.

I want everyone to repeat after me, "Are you sure you don't want to try again to fix it before we call someone?" I know everyone did not repeat after me, but I won't get hung up on it. This statement should be said prior to calling anyone. He knows you guys need to call someone, but it shows him you have faith in his abilities and won't let him give up too easy. Don't worry, when he's ready to call someone, nothing you say will be able to stop him.

Most men fail to realize that most women are very capable of fixing whatever is broken, except women have the good sense to know when they need to call in a professional. Men don't posses this sense. Eve ate that part of the apple first.

Men don't understand certain simple things, like, when the car needs to be washed, why women don't just get it washed? The trash needs to be taken out, then why can't the woman take it out? The dog needs to be walked, why can't the woman walk the dog? This list can go on and on, but I think the answer to all of these questions is simple. Men think they already do more than any woman and therefore should not have to do the simple things. After all, we are men and only work on the hard things.

Most men will always think that if his woman doesn't have an income-earning job and stays at home most of the time, then it's her job to do those things around the house. Change the bulbs, empty the trash, cook dinner, I know this is old-school thinking, but that doesn't make it any less true that your man will think this way.

To all the women who do have an income earning occupation, this is going to hurt - but the men in your life will always think their job is harder.

You could be a brain surgeon, him a taxi-cab driver and he'll still say his job is harder because he has to listen to people all day and you just have to put the person out and operate. You could be a roofer, and he'd say when he was in school he worked long, hot summers hauling roofing tiles - two bundles at a time, mind you - up a ladder all day long. It's your job to train him to stop thinking this way.

When my wife and I got married, we said if we could afford it, she would not work while we were raising children. After the birth of our first child, she left her job. I thought that her life was now easy because she didn't have a job. Wow, was I wrong.

My wife trained me and broke me of this way of thinking by not doing anything around the house for a week. Of course she would feed, change and bathe our son, but no dinner, no cleaning, no laundry for an entire week. Then she asked me to help her get caught up. Yes, she tricked me into thinking she was overwhelmed, but it worked. From that day forward I continued to think she had more work on a day-to-day basis then I did and on the weekends I would offer to help her with whatever needed to be done, unless it was football season. Then she only got me on Saturday - Sunday was all mine.

Okay, you've read this chapter and now I'm going to tell you something ALL men will deny. The real reasons men won't call in another to fix anything, besides the fact that it's usually the woman's suggestion; men are still pissed off from when women got the vote. Yes, we still have a 70 year animosity towards you having the right to vote in OUR elections.

Just kidding, but my wife bet me I wouldn't put that part in. She said I didn't have the gumption to do it.

I won; she lost, so sorry, too bad, now she has to pay up, I get a bone.

Chapter 8

I love you to Death...

Warning:

This is the most difficult chapter I have to write. It deals with why men beat their women. Why a man needs to hit, and act out violently against a woman. There will be no humor because this topic has no humor. As unpleasant as this chapter may be to read, it needs to be read and I need to say it. If you choose not to read this chapter, or feel you're unable to read it, skip to the next chapter. This topic might be too close to home for some. In the back of the book there are some resources for battered women which can help women become empowered to take action against the men who abuse women.

I want to start out by saying for the record, in no way, shape or form do I condone or approve of this behavior. I think it is the same as rape and should be treated as such. I have a request of any man who feels the need to hit a woman, please come to my house - I will put on a dress if it makes you feel superior, but remember: I hit back.

When a man rapes a woman, he is stripping her of her freedoms, her choice, her dignity and her life. Beating a woman does the exact same thing. It can take a very long time for a woman to recover from such a traumatic event.

If you're with a man who abuses you mentally or physically, leave him. I know it's not easy for some, but there are thousands of organizations setup to help. They can help move you, hide you, and feed you or whatever else you may need. They also help if you have children. They are out there, you just have to look.

Doctors will most likely disagree with me, but here is why men beat women.

From the time we're born, up through adulthood, men are taught we are stronger and better than women. We're supposed to be the boss, in charge and the king in our homes. What we say is law and the woman needs to obey without question.

Well, most people know this is a farce. Educated men and even those of us who are not so educated realize men and women have an equal say in a relationship.

Poorly raised and completely ignorant men who think that they must have the **last word** can be trained.

The man who knows better than to hit a woman, but still feels he must have **complete control** in a relationship, will beat his mate. If she doesn't listen, he acts out in a physical manner to get his way. This man should be locked away in jail and gang raped by the general population, all the while being told it's because he hits women. We should use the classical conditioning so that every time he thinks about hitting a woman, he also thinks about 100 men raping him.

I know women can push a man to the point where he thinks the only way to deal with her is to hit her. Women can really fuel the fire and then be surprised when it blows up. But, it is the man who should see the warning signs first. After all, it is his temper getting tried.

But sometimes a woman tends to ignore the signs when she sees them. I am in no way making excuses for men, I'm only pointing out that there are indeed warning signs and the women should learn to recognize them before he hits her. She should back off, if for no other reason than self-preservation.

The man must walk away. There is only one circumstance when I believe striking a woman is justified. It rarely ever manifests itself, but when it does, there is no other choice. Let me explain.

The only time striking a woman is justified is when she wields a weapon. Whether it is a gun, knife or bat, if she is coming after a man, he should have the right to defend himself. He should first try to remove himself from the area, but if that is not an option, he should disarm her, and then leave.

In the twenty plus years I've been married, I can say there was only one time I wanted to hit my wife, and I believe she knew it when I was at that point.

We had been married for just over a year, her mother was visiting and I agreed to take her mother to the airport when she left. Her flight was scheduled to leave around 4pm. I told her if we left around 2pm she would have no problem making her flight and she would also have some time to spare. She wanted to be at the airport by 2pm, so I agreed to take her at anytime she wanted.

My wife then asked if I was going to wait with her until her flight left, just in case it was delayed or cancelled. I told her that I don't wait for my dad's flights when he visits, I don't wait for my friends when they visit, so I wasn't going to wait for her mother at the airport all day for a "just in case."

She got very mad and began yelling at me. Some of the things she was saying were very out of character for her, but I think it was because her mother was there and she was trying to show her mother who the real boss of our relationship is. I yelled back and she hit me. Not hard, more like a shove, but at that point I told her I was leaving before I decided to hit her back. I walked out of the house and to my car; she followed me screaming the entire way. Her last words to me were, "Don't you walk away from me when I'm talking to you." I stayed in the car and yelled back, "If I don't leave, I'm going to knock you out. So I'm leaving instead. Don't wait for a call."

We have never had an argument get to that point since. That happened over twenty years ago. We talked the next day and she told me why she was so mad, and I told her why I was mad. But in our entire marriage, I have never hit her, and she has never hit me.

We have had arguments, but we both realize where our breaking point is and - more importantly – what the other's tolerance level is, so we tend to back off before we get there.

Some men can't do that. Some men can't back down to a woman. Also, they don't have the ability to recognize, acknowledge, and mitigate the fallout of reaching their own limits. These are the men you don't want. Leave them and find another. Don't waste your time on someone who is going to want to control your every move with violence.

There is plenty of help for those of you in an abusive relationship. Reach out to someone and ask. There are plenty of people willing to help any woman involved with a man who feels he has to dominate her through violence.

I knew a young girl involved with a guy who constantly beat her. She continued to make excuses for him telling me, "He really does Love me." We were at a company function one night and he showed up. Apparently he had not given her permission to go. He made no bones about hitting her in front of the crowd she was with. I was standing there.

I yelled for someone to call the police and I jumped on him. I was able to separate her from him and stood between the two of them to protect her. He tried to intimidate me with his muscles bulging and loud voice, but I just stood my ground kept him away from her.

Once I came to the realization he was not going to back down, I punched him right in the face. His last words were, "You can't protect her all the time." And he then got into his car and drove away.

The police showed, but she refused to press charges. This was when it was up to the battered person to press charges. Thankfully, most states have changed that law so the man can't intimidate the woman into not pressing charges.

I took her to her home and called my wife to let her know what just happened. I ask my friend if she wanted to stay the night at my house and in the morning we'd come back to her apartment and gather up her things. She said that wouldn't be necessary. I asked her to press charges and have him thrown in jail. She said it would only make things worse for her.

Two hours later he "loved her" into the hospital. I never saw her again.

Chapter 9

How do you Spell Commitment?...

Most women think men are afraid of commitment. We're not, we're more afraid of you asking us to spell it. Women think if their men won't live with them, then we must be afraid it. No, again, not only can we not spell it, we're afraid of what you're going to do to our apartment (refer to chapter 5).

The real reason is very simple. Man stems from the animal kingdom and, since most other animals are not monogamous, man thinks he is not required to be either. This is how we think. But there will be a time when all men are ready to settle down and take themselves out of the hunt. But until then, here's what we're thinking:

One day we'll be sitting in the bar when the twins show up. Yes, those all elusive twins only seen twice, never actually photographed in the wild. One guy was able to escape and tell his story, while the other guy didn't live to tell about it. Yes, those twins.

The twins show up and say, "Hi sexy, you want to come to our place and have no-strings-attached sex all night long?"I know, I know, but it's my book so let's get past it.

Although the chances of this happening are very slim, there is still a chance, and that chance is what keeps most men from taking the plunge into commitment. After all, it is the twins.

The twins usually show up the day after we commit to you. It always happens that way. Once we're off the market, they will appear just in time to let us know that our chances have been forever ruined. Most men will not stray once they make the decision to only be with you. However, there are many that will.

Agreeing to be sidelined and taken out of the game is a big step for men. Most men feel they have been pulled from the game too early, and some feel they've never had a real chance to play the game to the best of their abilities. This can cause friction between a man and woman. If a woman pushes a man to give up the hunt too soon, it can only cause problems later on and it will, in his mind, give him justification to cheat.

Speaking of the cheating, low life bastard he is, let's discuss some of the reasons for his actions, and notice I did not say excuses, I said reasons.

I don't think you can lay the blame on the woman for her man cheating, but I do think she should consider some of the reasons men cheat.

I've been asked by many of my women friends - why men cheat. After much thought, I have realized the reasons are as diverse as men are. I have narrowed it down to a few of the biggest and most common reasons. This is by no means a scientific test and should not be taken as such. It is just me asking the guys I knew had cheated and listening to their excuses. I didn't say reasons here because these guys use them as excuses.

A man would screw a light socket if he knew the electricity wasn't on, and some would do it if the electricity was on just to say they did it. That shows you our mind set - when it comes to sex. You have to understand that "love "and "sex" are very different. One is an emotion, which as explained before, is rolled up into the one single emotion of a man. The other, sex, is an act, much like eating a ham sandwich. Yes, I know what I said, it is seen the same in the minds of most men. We like it; we want it again, but on occasion we might want a turkey sandwich instead.

Men will usually cheat for physical reasons, while most women cheat for emotional reasons.

Men don't view sex the same as women and this causes tremendous confusion among the female population. Most men don't understand why women view sex the way they do and most women don't understand why men view it differently.

For a woman, sex is an expression or extension of the emotion of love. For men, sex is the benefit of having a steady girlfriend. It really is that simple. Most men love their mother, but they're not having sex with her. Men love a lot of things and - hopefully - they're not having sex with those things either.

Another reason for infidelity is insecurity. Men will often question why, - this beautiful, wonderful woman - is with them. Other men may not think she's beautiful, but because beauty is truly in the eye of the beholder, there is a man out there who thinks you're beautiful.

Insecurity kicks in and runs rampant with irrational thought. If a man sees a beautiful woman with another man, he immediately thinks that man must have either a lot of money, or, well, a high IQ. It couldn't be she likes him for who he is. No, that is unacceptable. He has a high IQ. But, if she's with him, he's The Man. IQ or not, he's Mr. Cool. This is just the way we think. We also know that another man could not possibly please her the way we could.

So here comes the insecurity part. Because we think this way, when she's with us, we're cool: if she's with him, she's a whore. We like whores - we know what we're getting and what it will cost with no strings attached. Plus, we don't have to remember her name.

It's a great boost to our ego if we can pick up a girl we think is out of our reach. All men know their limits and the range of obtainable women they can handle. But getting the big one is a dream, just like those twins. No man will ever admit openly he has limits, or that a particular woman might be out of his league, but inside we keep track and tally the score. For myself, I managed to marry far above my actual limitations.

On one hand we manifest delusions of greatness in our head, but then insecurity kicks in and we start questioning ourselves.

For myself, I know and believe there are plenty of women out of my league. I don't want to be what they want me to be. I won't compromise my values, morals or character to change into that which I am not. But there are plenty of men out there who will change at the drop of a light socket. My wife says I'm a bit different than most men. It took me a long time to understand who I am and what I want out of life.

If you don't believe me, ask my wife. I still have the same dreams I had when we were married, at least those that haven't been fulfilled. I still have great ambitions (and delusions) of world domination.

What does all this have to do with cheating? Well, if your man is not secure with himself, does not know who he is, how can he know what he wants? He can't and he doesn't. So he plays the field and continues to play after he is trapped in a relationship. The main reason he pretends to be with you only, is so he has access to a steady partner.

Insecurity can be recognized by an exaggerated display of machismo and testosterone. You have seen it - we all have seen it in some men. They try to exhibit self-confidence by being loud, opinionated and overbearing. These are usually the men who have no idea who they are. They are afraid someone will find out they are not what the world's vision of a man should be. I'm here to help you understand this, identify it and help your man over it.

There is another reason men cheat: impulse. Pure and simple, it's a spur-of-the-moment impulse. Sometimes that overwhelming impulse takes over and presto, the next thing we know, we're naked, screaming "Who's your Daddy" to some girl we just met. It affects both women and men.

Holding the man solely responsible for his indiscretion is unfair. Women have a small part in this also. Let me tell you a story to illustrate this.

You've been together for over one year; you've been living together a little less than that. You have an argument ending in both of you calling each other names. He knows he's not getting any treats from you tonight. While we're on the treats part, under no circumstances is it alright to withhold the treats. If you use your womanhood as a weapon, be warned, he will find it someplace else and not think twice about it.

When men argue with their woman, there is a certain amount of trust which is shared between them. They each trust the other is saying what they mean, and meaning what they say. But women have this great ability to talk around a subject, expect men to be mind readers, and then get pissed off when men don't know what the heck women are mad about. This destroys the trust and communication breaks down quick.

It takes a lot of unhappiness for women to cheat; it only takes a little for a man. When your conversations get to the point where the answers are only "yes" and "no" responses, step back and try to understand how both of you got to this point. Something is wrong and when there is something wrong, a man will look for physical comfort elsewhere. Doesn't make it correct, but it's a factor you have to consider.

Back to the argument, after all is said and done, he's going out and there is nothing you can do to stop him. Don't threaten to change the locks, it's still his apartment. Don't throw his stuff on the sidewalk and don't move out. Let him go blow off some steam with his buddies. This is a very vulnerable time for him. The nature of the argument and how mad he is has a direct impact on the odds of him picking up an anger screw.

Threatening to leave him is not a threat to him; it's a "get out of jail free" card that he might just use. Remember, men don't have the emotional depth women have and can make heat of the moment decisions that often the wrong decisions.

If you let him leave at the peak of the argument, you must at least say something like this before he is out of ear shot, "Call if you get too drunk to drive, I'll come get you" or maybe "I know we can work this out, when you're ready." It really doesn't matter what the argument is about at this point.

These statements show concern and compassion and let him know there is still someone at home waiting for him. He'll think twice about tapping that strange light socket.

You see, if you let him go in that state of mind, without letting him know there is a way to come back, you're inviting him to stray. He just left his "bitch" of a girlfriend and now has to prove to himself that he still has the ability to hunt. It's an anger management thing. Don't get me wrong, I'm not saying its right, it's not. However, it is a reason he'll use to justify his actions. Remember: don't let him leave without hearing a word of concern from you.

Men try to justify cheating with any excuse they can find, except the one that will prevent him from ever doing in the first place: trust. Trust between both of you is a huge part in preventing him from cheating. Trust he won't stray and chances are he won't. Trust he will stray, and he most definitely will, if for no other reason than you don't trust him anyway, so he can't break a trust which is not there.

At my bachelor party, my wife gave me permission to have one last taste of single life (I think she knew I wouldn't and that's why she gave me permission), I chose not to because I felt like this, if I wanted another woman, I shouldn't be getting married. If I wanted to play the field, I should not be in a serious relationship.

If you keep in mind that men don't think there is a direct relationship between love and sex, you'll understand him better. When he's caught and says, "but I love YOU" you'll understand he really doesn't see the connection between the two and chances are he really does love you.

I used to tell my wife, "Don't be afraid of me falling out of love with you; be afraid of me falling out of lust with you."

For men, there is no real emotional hurt when a woman cheats. For women, the hurt is very emotional. Wounds of the heart are far worse for women than men, and men don't understand that.

The bottom line is this, not all men cheat. Before you dump your man for cheating, you should try to find out why he strayed in the first place. If his behavior was motivated by no other reason than sex, dump him and get another.

He's not ready for any relationship at this point. However, if it is a breakdown in trust, work at it. He must be worth it, or you wouldn't have picked him to begin with.

Chapter 10
I'm Not Jealous, Just Crazy...

Everyone has some sort of minor insecurity caused by appearance, intelligence, and status of fortune or any number of other reasons. But in men, it's generally directly related to the size of their one-eyed friend.

The degree of insecurity will dictate the degree of a man's jealously, and vice a versa. One might say they are the same when it involves women. Jealous men have committed atrocities; they have conquered countries and lost them. They have gone to war - and pursued for peace. All this is done because of jealously. Some people call it envy; make no mistake, its pure jealousy. And for the record, all these involve a woman (I see a pattern here).

Men and women display jealousy in much the same way. So it should be easy for women to indentify it and know how to deal with in their man. But for some unknown reason, women think its funny and feed it when they see men struggling with it - wrong move.

Every man will get jealous to some degree. Generally that degree is directly related to the events being played out in front of him. Jealousy will feed on the man's imagination, and depending on how vivid a mental image he creates, he can explode into an uncontrollable rage. But that imagination is also directly related to insecurity. The more insecure your man is, the more vivid are the images of infidelity he imagines you are capable of. If your man is stupid, well, his images are of bunny rabbits and pretty puppies. No worries there.

If the man trusts his woman, even if he is very insecure, then his jealousy has little room to grow. This is because jealousy feeds on insecurity, but is starved by trust and self-confidence. Self-confidence is the opposite of insecurity. Trust and self-confidence are brothers. Jealousy can only manifest in an insecure man and one who has a low opinion of his value and worth.

The answer is simple: stay away from insecure men and you shouldn't have to deal with jealousy. If it were that easy, jealousy wouldn't have its own chapter. Not to mention that type of man who gets jealous all the time is probably living in his mother's basement, internet gaming and sucking down energy drinks by the case because he has zero social skills and has a name tape sewed into his underwear.

You want to be with a man who has some self-esteem, a bit of trust (you can earn what you need) and is not always fine when he sees you talking to another man.

I used to get jealous when I would see my wife talking with another man I didn't know. Not the kind of crazy jealous where a man walks up and says, "This is my girl, what are you doing with her?" No, not that kind of jealous, but I would ask her a lot of questions like, "Who was that?" and "What did he want?" The type of questions which sound accusatorial in nature and in tone.

It took me a long time to trust myself. I always trusted her, but it was the men she would talk to I didn't trust. That's because I know them, they are like me and I didn't trust "Me."

I never told my wife I felt this way. But as our relationship progressed, I became more secure with it. Now if I see her talking with a man I don't know, I don't add anything to it other than what it is: just talking.

If your man see's you talking to another man, he will automatically think the wrong thing. It doesn't matter how long you have been together, it's never going to appear innocent to him at first thought. He's going to want to know every word spoken. He might not come right out and say it, but he wants to know. So keep this in mind whether you are talking to an old friend, a new friend (which you're not allowed to have) or just someone excusing himself for bumping into you (not likely).

But if you see us talk to someone new, mind your own business, what, are you spying on us? Don't you trust us? Are you jealous?

Because men feel the need to acquire possessions, they also feel very protective of those possessions. So when your man see's you with another man, he starts to feel threatened and will have to take action. To counteract this behavior, reassure your man. Let him know that he is your only dog, give him a bone and tell him everything about the conversation. If you do this the first year you're together, you'll have gained the trust he requires to keep himself from going crazy jealous.

I know men who are extremely jealous. They see their women talking to another guy and go bonkers. Once they got her away from the unknown man, the inquisition would begin. They would rapid-fire questions at her - never waiting long enough for an answer. These guys also never maintained a long-term relationship.

Until this type of man can learn to trust women and gain more self-confidence, he will always have issues dealing with jealousy.

A long time ago, in a far off land (California), I knew these two people. Let's call them Adam and Eve.

Every night they would talk on the phone. Adam would call Eve and they would talk about each other's day, what the next day held in store for them and other boyfriend and girlfriend stuff, very cool and romantic. But when they were done talking, he made her keep the phone off the hook. This way he could hear her sleep. If she got up to go to the bathroom, he would ask her if everything was alright.

He did this every night for over one year. If she rolled over, he knew it, if she passed gas, he knew it. While she was sleeping, he would listen. He was such a light sleeper; he could hear everything going on in her bedroom. Now this was starting to get a little weird. But it persisted and she never said a thing to change it.

One night, she accidently hung up the phone. He went nuts. He got up, got dressed and went to her house. He started banging on the door until someone answered. By the way, she lived at home with her mother while she was going to college.

Her mother answered the door and gave him an ear-full for waking her up in the middle of the night. He caused such a racket; Eve woke up and came down stairs to see what was going on. When she saw Adam, she knew. She apologized for hanging up the phone by mistake. She claimed she went to the bathroom and when she passed the phone, she just reflexively hung it up. Adam didn't even try to call her back; he just went crazy and drove over as quickly as he could.

This was an eye-opener for Eve. A few weeks later, Eve broke up with Adam and explained to him she didn't want such a possessive relationship. Although Adam was crushed, he didn't freak out and beat her or do anything like that, but, he did have to let her go.

Adam was like that with every woman I knew he dated. I haven't seen him for over fifteen years, but I bet he is still single.

The more jealous your man is, the greater the chance you have of seeing him respond to situations with violence. I know a few women who love watching their men get jealous. This is dangerous. You would not pour fuel on a fire, why would you want to feed the jealousy of your man?

Remember to let him know that he can trust you, and that he has nothing to worry about if he see's you talking to another man. You do this by reminding him you're with him because he's smart, he's funny, you love his body, you know: lie to him.

After a few years, (or less if your man is not the jealous type), you should still remind him of his better qualities, but you don't have to worry about going out with your friends, making new friends or being able to talk to someone new without get the third degree.

Jealousy is a bitch to deal with, isn't it?

Chapter 11

From Man to Married...
(or Close to It)

Well, we're almost done training your man. Molding him into the man you want. Someone you can go out in public with and not get embarrassed. You know, your bitch.

There is no doubt in anyone's mind that's ever been married, marriage changes both people. I know firsthand. Believe it or not, you will change and so will he. I know this because I've seen it in Ripley's "Believe it or Not" museums. They have a marriage license hanging on the wall; next to it, is a plaque which reads, "How to turn your Princess into a Bitch."

But we're not ready for marriage just yet. I'm saving the marriage and beyond for my second book. I only bring up it here so you know I'm aware of the natural progression of relationships.

You still have little bit of training in store for him. You're going to train him not to be afraid of marriage.

Why do most men freak out at the prospect of marriage? They're terrified of the horror stories they've heard. For the most part, they only hear about the bad parts of marriage. The good is hardly ever mentioned, and the bad is usually true.

They've heard such terrifying stories; those stories make Steven King's books read like children's stories.

I believe most people are still getting married too young. They are in their twenties, just getting to know themselves. Instead of waiting until they are ready, they get married early because society programs us to do so.

It should also be harder to get a divorce. Most young people don't want to invest the time or energy it takes to build a great marriage. Divorce is a quick and easy way to not have to deal with couples issues.

I think people should live with each other for at least one year prior to marriage. This allows a sufficient amount of time to really get to know the other person. Living together exposes nuances and habits not seen in typical dating situations.

When you begin to live together, limits are set; rules and courtesies are extended in a way that is unnecessary in a casual relationship. If the rules are too much for the man, he always has an exit ready in the back of his mind. Since you're not married yet, the front door is still the easiest way out, for both of you.

Once you get married, the emergency exit is closed. The way out is further away and not so convenient any more. Men are afraid of this happening.

You have to train your man so the night after you're married, he doesn't have second thoughts. Remember, men go into marriage with the mindset that they will be the boss. They think they'll be in charge and make the rules now that you're married. If you have trained him well prior to this point, the transition will be easier, but not by much.

First you have to reassure him you're not going to quit your job once you're married. This is a big one for a man. It seems to most men that most women will quit working within the first three years of marriage. If you haven't discussed this with your man prior to getting married, then he will automatically assume you plan on stopping after you're married.

You have to talk it out with him and let him know of your plans, if you have any plans. If you don't plan on quitting work, let him know that also.

My wife and I talked about when she would stop working. We decided if we could afford it, she would stop when she got pregnant. If we couldn't afford it, she would continue to work provided the well-being of our children wasn't at risk. Both she and I believed there should be at least one parent at home with the children while they were growing up. It would be different once they got older, and she could go back to work if she chose to, or we needed her to. This would also be discussed by her and me at the correct time.

You should bring up this subject and see his response. When he rolls his eyes back into his head and falls face first into the table, you'll know it's too soon to get married. At least let his nose heal from the fall before you bring it up again. After a few broken noses, he'll come around.

You have to get him talking about children. This will open the door to discussing work issues. Talk about marriage, and the door is opened to discuss children. It doesn't really matter which way you go with this, marriage, then children, then work, or the other direction: work, children, and then marriage. But you have to get him talking about one of them before you can talk about the other.

Do not try to go too deep into each topic too quick. The natural course of the conversation will steer itself to each topic. With each topic he might fall over again so use caution when choosing the location to bring up the subject.

By the way, you should be done hanging junk in the hallway by now. You can start on the rest of the apartment.

Money is also a big issue with him. While you're both dating, money is never an issue. You earn and you spend. He earns and he spends. Once you're married, he's going to have issues with your spending habits, but not necessarily his own. Don't be insulted - it won't help and he won't care.

In the minds of most men, what he earns is his and what you earn is his. He's the man of the house and as such, gets to decide where the money is spent and - which is more important to him - on what. You and I know this is not true (I've been trained), but he doesn't know this yet.

You should discuss how the money will be handled once you're married. If both of you are working, you might suggest putting an equal amount into a joint account to pay the bills and what is left over; you get to do with the remainder as each of you pleases.

To broach the subject of money, you're going to need to gauge his reaction to you telling him you just spent two hundred dollars on a purse. Choose the location to tell him carefully; because he will pass out (I almost passed out writing this sentence).

The reaction he has will have a direct impact on how you suggest handling the finances.

You should suggest that his pay check be put towards the bills and yours will be for entertainment. But if you designate your pay for entertainment, you had better entertain. Trust me on this one; he'll hold you to it.

He's going to expect the money be handled the same way it is prior to marriage. He's going to be wrong. I know it and you know it, the trick is getting him to accept it prior to marriage.

One issue he'll have is sharing his stuff with you. Just in case you don't know, men don't like to share their stuff. The idea of everything you own becoming his is not a hard concept for him to digest, but the idea of his priceless artifacts of his bachelorhood becoming yours, well, it is just not going to happen. He knows that most of his stuff will end up in the trash or misplaced in unknown location never to be seen by human eyes again if he ever gives up total control of his possessions.

If you were successful in transforming his apartment into an "our place" from a "his place," then he shouldn't have too much stuff left hanging around you don't want anyway.

Then there is the "friends" issue to get him to accept. Remember what a marriage is, two parts coming together to form a single part. This concept is almost incomprehensible to men. Men are slow, but we're not stupid. We know one plus one doesn't equal one, it's two.

I look at it and think it makes three. I'll explain.

You have your life (that's one), he has his life (that's one) and until you get married, this equals two, but once you're married, you have created a combined life (that's one more) made from both of your individual lives. So if you add up all the ones, you get three after marriage. You shouldn't give up your life and your friends after marriage and neither should he, and he won't.

When he was single, whether or not you were living with him, if he wanted to go out with his friends, he would. He didn't need to consider you in the equation at all. Yes, I'm sure you noticed that even though you shared an apartment, his friends always seemed to come first.

Here's how we see it: we see you every day, we eat with you and we sleep with you. We don't look at it as a matter of priorities or the idea we should spend every minute with you, no, we see it more like a seniority thing.

Our friends have seniority over you. Get over it. We have known our friends longer; we have a special bond with them we don't share with you. We've been in fights with them and have been arrested with them. We have tried to pick up the same woman, and have lost the same woman to one another. We don't have to be proper when we're in public with them and we don't have to apologize to them for something we don't see as being wrong. There is a code among men which is, "never leave a friend behind" and the more important code, "If my friends don't run her off, she's a keeper," and this applies even in time of marriage.

So seniority has a lot to do with our choices. Your goal is to change that. It's not that hard to do, but you have to be willing to encourage him to go out with his buddies.

That's right, encourage him. Setting him free - will truly make him return.

You might suggest to him on Wednesday night that he call up his friends and go out on Friday night. It will throw him for a loop, but he won't feel like he is giving up his friends to be with you and his friends won't be threatened by your presence in their group. Make no mistake, it is their group.

The same holds true for your friends, but if you told him you were going out with your friends, I doubt he'd notice you were gone until he got hungry or horny. Speaking on that subject, never turn him loose to party with his friends when he's horny. Knock out a quickie before he leaves, then you send him out to have fun.

Your man will not understand why he should consider you when he is making plans with his friends. When you explain you might want to go out with them, the look on his face will tell it all. It never occurred to him you might want to go out with him and his friends. After a year or so, he'll start asking you if you want to party with them, but he won't ask all the time so don't expect him to. He still needs time with his friends without you, just as you should have time with yours without him.

Unfortunately, most men think our free time is just that, ours.

It is only through consistent training and behavioral modification that men will change. You must start the training process the moment you start dating. The old adage, "you can't teach an old dog new tricks," never held truer. I think it was a woman who coined that saying.

By now you're probably wondering why men are in your life at all; well, men often wonder the same thing about women.

Picking a good candidate for training is not rocket science. Here's a guide you can follow:

Most men between the ages of 21 and 30 have had on average, two steady relationships and approximately 10 to 14 one-night stands. This is the guy you can train. He has had some exposure to training and is still able to learn.

The man who has been through more than four steady relationships, and over 20 one-night stands in a nine-year period, is the one you need to stay away from. There is a definite relationship learning disability he suffers from. He doesn't seem to be able to retain the training as is readily apparent by the way women will not stay with him for long.

I'm not talking about dates, when I say one-night stands. I'm talking about playing house for the night with someone he just met. A man should have been on more dates - than sleepover's - if you can expect to be able to train him.

Well, we are at the end of his training. By now, you should be able to take him out in public, have the apartment filled with nice frilly things and weaseled your way into almost every aspect of his life without him ever knowing what happened.

I hope I was able to address most - if not all - of your questions. You now have basic tip s and techniques to start training any man you choose. Go fourth and pick a winner.

By the way, if you should see me in clubs or bars and it is obvious I'm on the hunt, please disregard the teachings of this book, sit down next to me and let's have a great time.

National women's shelters resources.

These are great places to find help in your area. They also help families.

http://www.safehorizon.org/
http://www.womenshelters.org/
http://www.sheltersforwomen.org/

Show off your man, visit our website for T-Shirts, Coffee Mugs, Hats and other great items.

www.menowner.com